Millions who see Mike Douglas on TV know him as one of the most decent, engaging personalities in the public eye. But almost no one knows the personal story of this veteran talk-show host and entertainer.

Now, master storyteller and filmmaker Mel White has probed beneath the surface and produced an inspiring eye-opener of a book.

Here for the first time is the secret of Mike Douglas's enduring success in the most volatile of all American businesses. *When the Going Gets Tough* is a tribute to the spiritual values that have sustained both the man and his marriage through more than three decades. It is also the story of bitterly disappointing setbacks, both personal and professional, and how Mike Douglas found the strength to persevere, survive, and ultimately thrive.

The resources that Mike Douglas lives by he also generously shares—in this warm, perceptive, uplifting narrative.

MEL WHITE is a noted film producer and author has traveled the world in search of stories that nee be told. His other books include *Margaret of Mol Deceived: The Jonestown Tragedy, The Other Si Love, In the Presence of Mine Enemies,* and *Teste Fire.* When not producing films, Dr. White is an ciate professor of communication and media minis at Fuller Theological Seminary.

Mel and his wife, Lyla White, have been writing and making films together for nineteen years. Alt she gives him the credit for their best-selling boo prize-winning film documentaries, he insist without her work as co-traveler, co-researcher, and critic, nothing would have been produce gether, they have produced two children as wel Kathleen and Michael Christopher.

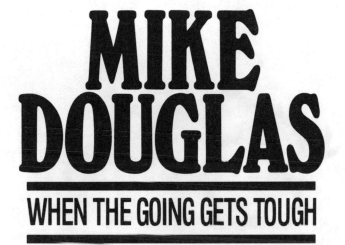

MIKE DOUGLAS

WHEN THE GOING GETS TOUGH

MIKE DOUGLAS

WHEN THE GOING GETS TOUGH

MEL WHITE

WORD BOOKS
PUBLISHER
WACO, TEXAS

MIKE DOUGLAS: WHEN THE GOING GETS TOUGH

Library of Congress Cataloging in Publication Data:

White, Mel, 1940–
  Mike Douglas—when the going gets tough

  1. Douglas, Mike.   2. Television personalities—United
States—Biography.   3. Singers—United States—Biography.
4. Christian biography—United States.   1. Douglas,
Mike.   II. Title.
PN1992.4.D58W48   1982   791.45′092′4   B   82-15991
ISBN 0-8499-0318-1

Quotations used in chapter epigraphs are from the following sources:

CHAPTER 1: Lillian Carter and Gloria Carter Spann, *Away from Home: Letters to My Family* (New York: Simon and Schuster, 1977), pp. 121–122. CHAPTER 2: Eric Lax, *On Being Funny: Woody Allen and Comedy* (New York: Charterhouse, 1975), pp. 224–225, 232. CHAPTER 3: Joseph P. Blank, *Nineteen Steps Up the Mountain: The Story of the DeBolt Family* (Philadelphia: J. P. Lippincott, 1976), p. 8. CHAPTER 4: Interview with Carol Burnett, *Good Housekeeping* 180, no. 2 (February 1975): 72, 129; "Carol Burnett's Own Story," *McCall's* 105, no. 5 (February 1978): 126. CHAPTER 5: Margot Fonteyn, *Margot Fonteyn, Autobiography* (New York: Warner Books, 1975), pp. 25, 306. CHAPTER 6: Winthrop Griffith, *Humphrey: A Candid Biography* (New York: Wm. Morrow and Co., 1965), p. 216. CHAPTER 7: Malcolm Muggeridge, *Something Beautiful for God: Mother Teresa of Calcutta* (Garden City, NY: Image Books, div. of Doubleday & Co., 1971), pp. 65, 80. CHAPTER 8: Interview with Ray Charles, *Ebony* 29, no. 12 (October 1974): 125, 132, 134. CHAPTER 9: Norman Vincent Peale, *The Power of Positive Thinking* (New York: Prentice Hall, 1952), p. 39. CHAPTER 10: Lawrence Welk, *This I Believe* (New York: Prentice Hall, 1979), pp. 190–191. CHAPTER 11: Billy Graham, "Building Bridges," *Saturday Evening Post,* February 1980, p. 75. CHAPTER 12: *Newsweek,* 16 June 1980, p. 63.

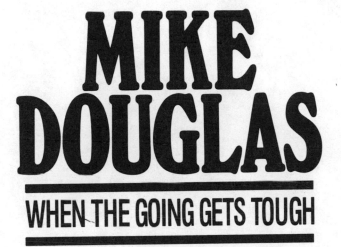

MIKE DOUGLAS

WHEN THE GOING GETS TOUGH

We often take "The Mike Douglas Show" on the road to interview people who for various reasons cannot come to our studios. I'll never forget visiting Plains, Georgia, not long after her favorite son was elected President of the United States. Although I interviewed President Carter that day, my lasting memories of that visit still center on the interview with his mother, Miss Lillian. At the age of seventy she volunteered to work with the Peace Corps in India. She shared with me some of her experiences there, and I'll not soon forget them.

MIKE DOUGLAS

Sometimes, I think my coming to work in India with the Peace Corps was a completely selfish move. I left all personal worries behind me, and went to another world, where my worries are not personal but of such huge proportions that it takes more than just me to overcome them. So, I say, "Come on, God, this is Your problem!" And He answers. I didn't dream that in this remote corner of the world, far away from the people and material things I had always considered necessary, I would discover what life is really all about. Sharing yourself with others, and accepting their love for you, is the most precious gift of all. If I had one wish for my children, it would be that each of you would dare to do the things and reach for goals in your own lives that have meaning for you as individuals, doing as much as you can for everybody, but not worrying if you don't please everyone.

LILLIAN CARTER

Chapter One

THE UNIFORMED CHAUFFEUR nodded politely to Mike and Genevieve Douglas as they stooped to enter the Daimler-Benz limousine. The doorman of the Ritz saw his special guests comfortably settled into the posh leather and teakwood interior and then smiled down on them.

"Bon voyage!" he said, closing the rear door almost noiselessly. "You will love the Queen Elizabeth II. She's the greatest ship afloat, you know."

He winked with British pride and tipped his top hat with a flourish. A traffic bobby halted the busy flow of automobiles and double-decker buses moving past the hotel's grand entrance and waved the Douglases' limousine onto Grosvenor Place. They rode as royalty through the streets of London, across the River Thames, past Waterloo Station, and down Brixton Road towards Southampton Port two hours away.

There, towering thirteen decks above the water line, waited the QEII, rightly described as the last great ship to sail the North Atlantic—flagship of the Cunard Line, pride of all Britannia. It was December 4, 1981. For the next six days Mike and Genevieve Douglas would live and work in the splendor of a floating city as the QEII made her last transatlantic crossing of the season. During the voyage, five hour-long television specials would be taped for the "Mike Douglas Entertainment Hour."

9

Already, Mike's celebrity guests, his orchestra, his television crew and personal production staff had boarded the QEII. The impressive two-story salon or Double Down Room, the center of the great ship's social life, had been lit with powerful television lights. Wires had been strung, microphones tested; dressing rooms, rehearsal areas, and a fully equipped video-control center had been prepared. This cruise, the Queen would be a floating television studio.

From December 11, 1961, when the "Mike Douglas Show" was born in Cleveland, Ohio, until June of 1980, Douglas had consistently been the most popular and most viewed day-time talk-and-variety-show host in the nation. Tens of millions of loyal viewers had watched every day as Douglas interviewed the biggest names in show business, politics, literature, sports, and religion—people like Fred Astaire and Gene Kelly, Elton John, Billy Graham and Archbishop Sheen, Paul Simon, John Wayne, Marlon Brando, Princess Grace, Jimmy Stewart, and James Michener. Presidents and kings, dictators and freedom fighters had been counted among his more than four thousand guests, interviewed on remote locations from Moscow to Mexico City, from Monte Carlo to Miami. Now in the new "Entertainment Hour" format, his Emmy-award-winning television presence had been a major part of America's television habit for a record-breaking twenty years.

Mike Douglas had been a television star of such long standing that in the celebrity-studded receiving line at the White House the President's wife, Lady Bird Johnson, had reached out to shake Douglas's hand and exclaimed, "At last, a familiar face." Now, as word spread among the passengers of the QEII, many long-time fans lined the open decks and stateroom windows, hoping to see Mike Douglas as he came on board.

The Daimler limousine sped through the grazing lands of Southern England, completing its journey to Southampton. Mike and Gen Douglas chatted quietly about the cruise, reviewed the elaborate taping and rehearsal schedules, and dozed intermittently. Mike Douglas looked at his watch with the controlled nervousness of a professional entertainer who had counted down the clock on more than six thousand personally produced television hours. He read, then reread, the departure time printed on his travel itinerary.

"How long before we arrive at the docks?" he asked the driver through the limo intercom system.

"Don't worry, sir!" the driver answered, looking back over his shoulder reassuringly, "The Queen won't sail without you."

Douglas smiled and whispered, "I thought the British understated."

Gen took his hand, lay back against the suede-soft leather seat, and laughed quietly.

"It might be true, Mike. This one time the Queen just might wait."

They rode awhile in silence, sharing the nervous excitement they had known together for almost four decades of loving partnership. Mike and Genevieve Douglas are truly unique. Her name has never appeared in the title credits of any of his television productions. She has insisted on anonymity, even though her husband describes her as "my loyal partner, most valuable asset, intuitive, skilled, a true professional in the entertainment crafts." To have maintained their close working relationship in such a tough trade so long and so successfully is a phenomenon almost unknown in show business history, but to have maintained their marriage as well over those almost forty years in perhaps the most competitive and marriage-busting business on earth is more unusual still. In the limousine that day, they both blushed slightly and looked chagrined as they shared the almost unbelievably rapid and spontaneous chain of events that led to their long-term marriage partnership.

"Gen, would you read the next page from A Tale of Two Cities?" *Genevieve Purnell sat daydreaming in her sixth period lit class. When her teacher called on her to read, Gen didn't even look back from the window out of which she had been gazing while other classmates read.*

"Gen?" chided the teacher. "Are we interrupting something? Let's not keep Charles Dickens waiting!"

Classmates giggled. The teacher smiled understandingly. Gen

*blushed and fumbled through her textbook, trying to recall
where the reading had ended. It is normal for high-school-senior
minds to wander occasionally on fine spring days, but that entire
academic day had been wasted on Gen Purnell. In just two
short hours, she would change her name forever. She said the
new name over to herself, savoring the sound of it: Mrs. Michael
Delaney Dowd, Jr.*

*A loud buzzer sounded in the hall just outside the classroom
and students rushed for lockers, gyms, the library, malt shops,
after-school jobs, and homework. For the first time, Genevieve
Purnell led the pack away from Classen High School, her heart
pounding as she ran the ten blocks to her home on Southwest
Twenty-Second Street. Racing up the front stairs to her bedroom,
she slipped off her penny loafers, removed her skirt and blouse,
and piled her school clothes neatly on the bed. Quickly she
put on her patent leather heels from Kerr's Department Store
and her blue Sunday suit with its white collar and white lace
cuffs, and in record time she was out the front door, running
down the street toward an unknown future.*

*As she rushed from the house, her bridegroom was hurrying
just as excitedly towards the nearby home of his friends, Harold
and Winifred Betts—a dozen red roses in his arms and a beautiful platinum ring in his pocket. Michael Delaney Dowd, Jr.
was eighteen, a staff singer at Radio Station WKY in Oklahoma
City. Harold, a pianist/singer at WKY, and his wife, Win, had
offered their help in the urgent matter at hand, and they were
waiting for him as he bounded up the steps. He ducked behind
the front door, his arms full of roses, and waited to surprise
young Genevieve as she rushed up the stairs and into his life
forever.*

*He wasn't far ahead of her. Ankles wobbling in high heeled
shoes not meant for running, she ran up the walk and up to
the door, flinging it open with such force that she nearly broke
Michael's nose. Then they crushed a dozen roses between them
in the blind excitement of their embrace.*

*"Hey, easy on the flowers, kids," Harold laughed, leading
his teenaged friends to the old Packard standing ready in the*

driveway. "They have to last through the ceremony, you know."

Joking and talking, they piled into the Packard, then fell strangely silent as Harold backed it out of the driveway and pointed it towards nearby Norman, Oklahoma and a justice of the peace. It was April 6, 1943.

"Actually, it wasn't a very convenient time to fall in love," remembered Mike as their limousine rolled across the English countryside. "In November of 1942, when we first met, World War II was at a significant turning point. Hitler's armies were in retreat. The Fuhrer's Luftwaffe and submarine forces were losing the battle for control of the Atlantic, and massive shipments of arms and ammunition were steaming towards Southampton and other British ports. The inevitable allied invasion of Europe was being prepared in these very fields." He pointed out the limo window at the passing view.

"I was eighteen then," he confessed. "In six short months I would be wearing a uniform of the United States Navy, serving as a communication officer on one of those ships sailing towards Southampton with ammunition for the invasion of France. But right then, in November, World War II seemed far away. I was in Oklahoma City, freshly arrived from Chicago for my first real job in broadcasing."

"And I was only sixteen," added Gen. "My brother, Charles Purnell, wrote continuity copy at WKY. When Mike arrived from Chicago, my brother liked him immediately and took him under his wing. It was Thanksgiving, and Michael had planned on eating his usual lunch in a nearby drugstore. He didn't know my brother Charles's determination.

" 'Nobody eats Thanksgiving dinner in a drugstore,' Charles told Mike, and with no further argument he escorted Michael Dowd, Jr. away from WKY, across Oklahoma City and directly into my mother's fragrant kitchen. That was the first moment of our life together," Gen remembered. "He stood in the doorway shaking hands with my father. My mom hurried across the kitchen to take his coat and make him feel welcome. I was standing near the open oven basting the turkey, and I could see Mike over my shoulder, just standing there, staring at me."

"She looked up at me," Mike remembered, "brushing the long chestnut-colored hair from her eyes with her forearm. Her hands were white with flour from a pie crust she had been rolling and she smiled a schoolgirl smile at me that stopped me dead in place.

" 'Hello, Michael,' she said, and I loved her. That was it. I never doubted from that moment that sixteen-year-old Genevieve would one day be my bride, or that we would share our lives together.

"After that first Thanksgiving introduction," Mike added, "I watched Gen on every possible opportunity. On lonely Friday evenings at the local high-school stadium, when I found myself at the only game in town, I watched Gen in her double-knit COMET sweater cheering nearby in the crowd. I chatted with her on visits with Charlie to the Purnell home. I sipped cokes at a donut shop near her high school, hoping she would walk by, chestnut hair gleaming, and wave or smile at me as she passed. I was hopelessly in love, so hopelessly that I didn't even manage to ask her out . . ."

"Then came my seventeenth birthday," Gen remembered. "A pageboy at WKY had invited me to spend an evening at the station as his date. I was wearing an expensive purple orchid he had bought me for the occasion and following him dutifully through the different studios and rehearsal rooms of WKY. Then Michael wandered into the record library and saw us chatting there."

" 'Hey, Bobby,' I called to the page," Mike added. " 'Do you mind grabbing the red folder of sheet music in the library for me and delivering it to Studio B? I'm running late.' "

" 'Sure, Michael,' the page answered me. 'Excuse me, Gen,' he mumbled and was gone. I felt guilty making up such a lame excuse to get rid of her date. It was wrong, but I was in love."

"He walked over to me," Gen said, describing her memories

of that moment, "and I reached into my purse on some pretense to avoid his eyes. I stood fumbling there, thrown by his sudden, silent presence.

" 'Gen,' he whispered finally, 'When this war is over, will you marry me?'

"I looked up at him, thinking he was joking. Then I saw immediately that he was very serious. So it was my turn to stare incredulously at him."

"I've never seen a look like that in any other woman's eyes," added Mike. "I can remember it to this day thirty-eight years later."

"After a long awkward silence I answered him as directly as he had asked," remembered Gen. " 'Yes, Michael, I will marry you.' "

"We had never talked of marriage," said Mike. "We had never really dated! And World War II seemed a million miles away. Then the page returned, his arms full of folders, and whisked Genevieve away.

"Five months later," Mike continued, "I was classified 1-A and ordered to report for induction into the United States Navy. For the first time," he confessed, "I began to put down sheet music and pick up the teletype accounts of battles in such exotic places as Stalingrad and El Alamein, Burma and Truk. As I vocalized in the rehearsal room, I would turn up news reports of Hitler, Rommel and Goering, Eisenhower, Montgomery and de Gaulle. In those last twelve months, German U-boats had sent 6,250,000 tons of allied shipping torpedo-blasted to the bottom of the sea. Suddenly, it dawned on me that one day soon I would be on one of those same liberty ships sailing in those same blood-and-oil-covered waters, to those same war-ravaged ports. Though I didn't feel afraid, I knew I could not wait until the war was over to marry Genevieve."

They drove the twenty miles to nearby Norman in silence— at least no one remembers saying anything. They entered the office of a justice of the peace near the Oklahoma University campus, hoping to look as old and experienced as any of the college seniors walking on the campus nearby.

"Do you, Genevieve Purnell, take this man, Michael Delaney Dowd, Jr., to be your lawfully wedded husband, to have and to hold from this day forth till death do you part?"

"I do," answered Gen, standing on tiptoe and looking into Michael's eyes.

"Do you, Michael Delaney Dowd, Jr., take this woman, Genevieve Purnell, to be your lawfully wedded wife, to have and to hold from this day forth till death do you part?"

"I do," answered Michael, a bit concerned about the "lawfully" part but bluffing it through with all the calm bravado that would sustain him through a lifetime of television pressure.

"Then by the authority invested in me by the state of Oklahoma, I pronounce you man and wife. You may kiss the bride."

It was a quick kiss and a quicker getaway. Harold and Win Betts signed as witnesses. Hurriedly, Mike paid the justice's fee and rushed everybody towards the door, fearing that at any minute someone might come in and say, "Hey, you kids can't get married." But they made it safely down the steps, and they whipped that old Packard back toward Oklahoma City at top speed.

For a moment Mike and Gen Douglas sat without speaking in the limousine as they entered the village of Southampton and headed towards the huge docking area. Then Gen spoke.

"I feel a bit foolish, even now when I remember it," she said. "I'm afraid people will say, 'They didn't know what they were doing, those two young kids, to run away and get married,' and in so many ways they would be right.

"We didn't know what lay ahead. We didn't know the years of hardship and sacrifice we faced. We never dreamed of the long separations and lonely nights and empty refrigerators and depleted checking accounts awaiting us. We didn't have a marriage counselor. We didn't even tell my pastor or Mike's priest. Both his parents and mine suspected we were in love, but

how we had the courage to get married, lie to the justice of
the peace about our ages, and forge changes on the marriage
license is still a mystery, a wonderful unbelievable mystery
that only God could understand."

Mike listened and nodded as Gen reminisced. Then he added,
"Whatever the critics might say of that lovely, lonely, spontaneous act, I would do it all again without a moment's hesitation.
We were in love, and with that love came a kind of commitment
to each other that we knew would be forever. And when commitment is forever," Mike added, "why not let forever begin
today?"

The limousine driver was cleared to enter the harbor area.
In the distance the QEII rode proudly at her pier, smokestacks
gleaming in the later afternoon sunlight.

"Oh, yes," added Gen, "we musn't forget my mom's reaction
to that brief hour we were missing."

"How could I forget what she said to us that day?" added
Mike. "Or that strange look on her face as she looked me
right in the eye and said it?

" 'Where have you two been?' she asked. 'You didn't go
off and get married did you?' "

"But we had decided not to tell either of our parents right
away," Gen added. "And it got us into trouble almost immediately. That evening my family gathered in the breakfast room,
snacked, and played a game of cards, with both of us dying
to be alone and absolutely confounded as to how it might be
accomplished."

"Finally, Dad Purnell took out his pocket watch," remembered Mike. "Winding it was a signal that the evening was
ending, and we both sighed with relief. Then Gen's dad did
the unexpected.

" 'Well, Mike,' he said, 'it's getting late.' He stood to his
feet and gently led me to the door. 'You must be tired after
singing all day.' He added, 'You have to watch that voice,
you know.'

"I looked at Gen helplessly as her dad headed me out the
door and down the stairs. Both of her parents were smiling

and waving from the porch. I've never forgotten that awful moment," Mike recalls, "and I never let Dad Purnell forget it either. Years later I would remind him, 'Remember, Dad, when you sent me home on my wedding night without even a goodnight kiss?'

" 'Yes,' he always answered on cue, chin up for effect and grinning broadly, 'I didn't want you to miss the last bus.' "

The huge entry building was almost empty when the limousine arrived in Southampton. Quiet prevailed where only hours before the boat train from London and hundreds of taxis and buses had pulled in, disgorging excited passengers about to embark on North Atlantic or round-the-world cruises. A thousand crewpersons had hurried back from shore leave, ready to man every station on the liner from the dog kennels on boat deck to the hospital and health club ten decks below. Now, only a few stevedores remained on duty with their pushcarts in hand; tons of luggage had already been stored in the ship's giant holds as passengers were scooped up by escalators into the huge waiting room and entry hall on the pier beside the liner.

Hundreds of scotch eggs and tomato sandwiches had been eaten, and a small river of lager beer and East India tea had been drunk as more than a thousand passengers passed through the smiling cordon of Cunard ladies in blue uniforms who were checking passports and tickets, issuing boarding passes and souvenir carry-on bags. Now, at the bottom of one escalator, in the almost eerie silence of the huge hall, stood a handful of Cunard officials and a few of the bobbies who had directed the flow of human traffic to and from the ship. Ernie DiMassa, Mike Douglas's producer for more than a dozen years, and Lynn Faragalli, Mike's personal secretary, stood with them.

Ernie DiMassa, six foot, six inches tall, wore a long fur coat and stood motionless, staring darkly at the entry for the Daimler-Benz limousine that would bring Mike and Gen Douglas down from London. Lynn Faragalli, short and exuberant, stood at his side, with her boss's boarding passes in hand, waiting to join the Cunard officials in whisking them through customs and onto the waiting liner.

The Daimler-Benz appeared just as the official police band, in scarlet tunics and silver-topped black bobby hats, began to play. Mike and Gen were escorted by their entourage up the escalator into the entry hall, through the customs check, and toward their suite on the QEII. A remote television crew recorded the first moments of their arrival and boarding of the QEII.

The Trafalgar Suite is high above the ship on Signal Deck and has two floors connected by a private stairway. The television production staff waited in the living room on the first floor of the suite. There were dozens of important decisions to be made, schedules to be arranged and rearranged, scripts to be written and rewritten and memorized, songs and dances and routines to be learned. But for one last quiet moment Mike and Gen Douglas, in their upstairs living quarters, were alone together. Mike pushed open the door leading out onto their private balcony high above the sea. By now it had grown dark, and the cool night air carried the sound of trumpets and drums across the harbor. Gen put on a sweater and stepped out beside her husband. They stood side by side, watching the lights shimmering on the water, saying nothing.

So much had happened since that day in Norman, Oklahoma, when two love-struck teenagers pledged their lives to each other forever. So much would happen in the next six days of production as they sailed to New York City four thousand miles away. And the next ten years were already being scheduled and shaped by these two dreamers and their production plans. But that one moment they had to themselves— just the two of them, together. They stood, arms touching, feeling each other's love. Smoothly, almost imperceptibly, the QEII began its journey. Mike and Genevieve Douglas were on the road again.

In the past two decades of show business I have interviewed all the great comics from Charlie Chaplin to Woody Allen. We tend to underestimate the role of laughter in our lives. Jesus spoke humorously to life's most important issues. He told stories about men with logs in their eyes trying to remove a speck of sawdust from the eye of another. It would be as difficult for a rich man to enter heaven, Jesus warned, as for a camel to pass through the eye of a needle. He used humor to break past his listener's defenses and make them think seriously about life's most complex problems. So do the great comics of our time. On the surface, they may seem frivolous or lightweight, but in fact the laughter they produce in us is the first step in confronting us with the issues we spend a lifetime trying to suppress and deny.

MIKE DOUGLAS

It is possible to experience one's own death objectively and still carry a tune.

Death is one of the few things that can be done as easily lying down.

I do not believe in an afterlife, although I am bringing a change of underwear.

Also, there is the fear that there is an afterlife, but no one will know where it is being held.

It's not that I'm afraid to die. I just don't want to be there when it happens.

I don't want to achieve immortality through my work. I want to achieve it through not dying.

WOODY ALLEN

Chapter Two

MIKE DOUGLAS STOOD ON THE ALMOST-DESERTED DECK of the Queen Elizabeth II, breathing the salt air and listening appreciatively to the slap of waves against the ship's hull far beneath him. It was getting late. His meeting with cast and crew had long since broken up, and activity on board had slowed to a standstill. He knew that soon he needed to go upstairs, where Gen sat waiting for him in their private quarters. They both needed a full night's rest to get through the demanding days ahead.

But right now sleep was the farthest thing from his mind. His usually accurate cerebral clock had lost nine hours on the British Air DC10 polar flight to London from Los Angeles. While Cunard stewards and stewardesses were folding down covers on stateroom beds and laying out late-night cups of tea or bouillon, Douglas was ready for breakfast. It seemed strange to walk the oakwood-paneled stairways to the boat deck below knowing that a thousand other passengers were sleeping when he felt wide awake.

Then again, it wasn't unusual for him to experience sleeplessness just before an important videotaping, especially if the program didn't feel just right. While cast and crew slept, Douglas often stayed awake, arranging and rearranging a program's pieces until finally the picture seemed complete. Tonight's meeting had gone well, however, and the plans for the next day's shooting looked good.

Perhaps he wandered the decks just from sheer excitement—the delight of being back at sea again. This transatlantic voyage on the QEII was not Mike's first time to perform afloat. In fact, his love of ships and sailing began in his early teen years, when he spent his summers entertaining passengers on cruise ships day-sailing on Lake Michigan.

Leaning against the deck rails of the QEII, Mike peered down at the dark water as he relived his memories of those early days. . . .

"Look at that great ship," said Mrs. Dowd as they hurried hand in hand from the bus stop on Chicago's Lakeside Drive toward the old Diversey Harbor. "Imagine my own little Michael singing to all those fine ladies and gentlemen."

"Mom," retorted Michael, "it's a rickety old tub, and the passengers are probably a bunch of Iowa tourists who'll get seasick and throw up while I'm singing."

"You'll be singing, Michael Dowd," his mother said breathlessly, "and tub or no tub, you'll be singing like an angel."

She said it like a threat, and Michael nodded and bounded up the gangplank in obedience to that threat. Actually, he was as excited as she was—at fourteen, he was about to earn his first "big money" as a singer. A funny-looking "angel" in blue pants, red-and-white-striped jacket, and yellow straw Panama hat, he walked the gangway that day with a thrill equal to boarding the QEII.

"Sure, it was a nothing little steamer on Lake Michigan," remembered Mike with a grin, "with a nothing little band that played so loud it was hard to sing above it, but with hat in hand I sang "Danny Boy" and all the other Irish songs my mother had taught me. It was a wonderful experience, and the passengers would tip us as they strolled the decks, or smile and say, 'That was nice. Sing it again.' "

Singing was a dream his mother had had for him from his

earliest childhood, and Michael Delaney Dowd, Jr. had been captured by her dream.

"Mom was very loving and very demonstrative. She liked to make people happy. She had a beautiful soprano voice and the spark of a natural entertainer. But her parents saw show business as a career far too outlandish for any respectable woman, let alone their lovely little daughter. So when Mom saw that spark of an entertainer in me, she fanned that spark until it flamed. She was never one of those notorious 'stage mothers'; she was more relaxed in her ambitions for me. But she did work hard to make it possible for me to fulfill my dreams of becoming a singer."

Actually it was the Catholic grade school Mike attended that can be credited for discovering Michael Delaney Dowd, Jr., would-be Irish crooner. Mike wanted to play football and basketball in those days. He was quick and sure-footed, but he was also short and, even then, tall was in. He didn't feel the heady excitement of grammar-school fame until that morning in music class when a tall, "hatchet faced" nun leaned down in his direction while the six-year-olds were practicing for their Christmas program.

"She stopped right in front of me," Mike recalled, "and stared at me while we sang. I knew I was in big trouble but I couldn't figure out why."

The nun cupped her hand over one ear and awkwardly got down on her knees in front of him, straining to hear his voice above the others. Finally, the song ended.

"Michael Dowd, is it?" she asked him.

"Yes, sister," Mike answered, fearing the wrath of God from this stern-looking nun in wimple and habit.

"You're a singer, then?" she asked.

"No, sister. I mean, yes, sister."

"Then she smiled," remembers Mike, "took me gently by the shoulder to her desk and sat me down beside it."

"God has given you a voice, Michael Dowd. It isn't a great voice yet, but it will do for the solos in this year's Christmas pageant."

With that beatific announcement, Michael began his career. His mother took care of the rest. When he was only eight years old she took him to an audition for a popular Chicago radio show, the WLS Barn Dance Review. . . .

The judge looked up from his clipboard. "Mrs. Dowd?" He smiled at the attractive woman with the tiny boy in short pants— the boy who had belted out those Irish ballads in a clear child soprano.

"I think we can use you, Michael," he said. "Mrs. Dowd, if you'll just come into the office, we'll sign the contract, and then we'll be on our way."

They followed him into the next room.

"By the way, Mrs. Dowd, how old is little Michael?"

Michael's mother looked down at the floor, then up at her son.

"He's eight, sir," she stammered. She couldn't lie, even if it meant losing the contract—which it did.

"Mrs. Dowd, you know about the child labor laws. We can't have an eight-year-old working here. I'm sorry."

With that, the contract was taken back out of Mrs. Dowd's hands. She just sat there a moment without speaking. And little Michael felt worse for her—much worse—than he felt for himself. It was a chance at show business, and one little lie could have meant his first big break. But his mom couldn't, wouldn't lie.

Mrs. Dowd stood slowly, thanked the gentlemen politely, took young Michael's hand, and walked from the WLS studio to the bus stop nearby.

"I'm sorry, Michael," she said. And then she stopped, got down on one knee in front of him, took his shoulders in her hands, and said, "But I have another plan. Listen. . . ."

There was always another way for Mrs. Michael Delaney Dowd, Sr. She rushed Michael home and began to sew matching costumes for Mike and a neighbor boy, Rusty Gill. They both played guitar, at least a bit. They both could sing, at least a bit. And so she produced the first singing team from that tough neighborhood, and got it booked into birthday parties and bar mitzvahs, mom-and-pop-store openings, and old ladies' teas. They were Michael and Rusty, the Singing Schoolboys. And day after day she rehearsed them on such classics as "Shine On Harvest Moon" and "I'm Looking Over a Four-Leaf Clover." They both played chords on guitar strings their little fingers could hardly cover. Rusty crooned the melodies—because only Michael could sing harmony. And Mrs. Dowd sat cheering on the sidelines.

On Saturday mornings Michael's mother would take him on the number-four bus downtown to the great Chicago Theater on the loop. Mom and son would be the first in line for front-row tickets. They sat through the feature or the serial film. Then, as the spotlight blazed down on the mighty Wurlitzer pipe organ, Mom Dowd would take Michael's hand and whisper, "Shh, Michael, listen. It's time."

"Those great pipes would sound their fanfare and the snare would roll from somewhere far away and the announcer would bellow into the microphone, 'Ladies and gentlemen, Jimmy Dorsey and his band.' I could feel Mother's excitement flowing into me. I could feel the energy in her as that great stage rose in front of us with the Jimmy Dorsey band playing at full volume. It was magic. We both leaned far over the rail and watched the musicians playing as the orchestra pit reached eye level. I could see my Mom's eyes brim with tears of excitement as the music flowed over and around us. And the smile of happiness she radiated down at me as we both applauded wildly was a smile that cut the darkness of the Depression, of growing up in the poverty in old Chicago, of being a little guy in a big guy's world. It made me happy too.

"One Saturday morning a young soloist sang with the Dorsey Band. He wore brown and white shoes, brown pants, and a tan coat with wide lapels and enormous shoulders. His dark, greased hair shone in the spotlight, and as he began to sing the girls, squealing with delight, rushed the stage. I even remember the song he sang that day—'The Breeze and I.' The crowd went wild. Everybody was on their feet clapping and laughing and shouting for more.

"And I thought, wow," remembered Mike, "that's exactly what I want to do. I want to stand in front of that big band. I want to wear a brown suit with enormous shoulders. I want to sing and make people happy."

"Mom," he asked as they waited for the bus that day, "do people get paid for coming out on the stage and singing like that?"

"Yes, son," she answered. "They get paid a lot."

"And I stood there thinking, 'To make people happy and get paid for it—what could be a better job than that?' "

Michael's father didn't like the idea one bit. He wanted Michael out on the football field with his older brother, Bob. He wanted Mike tough and street-ready. Michael Delaney Dowd, Sr. was a freight handler for the Canadian Pacific Railroad. The Dowds lived in a racially mixed section of old Chicago during the Depression and the post-Depression years. Mike remembers that his family never felt poor because "no one around us had anything either." The Dowd family moved often and never really had a family home. Senior Dowd made fair money as a freight handler, but he loved the horses almost as much as he loved a pint of good Irish Stout at Rafferty's pub.

Mr. Dowd had two older brothers who were both over six feet tall, but Dowd himself was only five feet, five inches. "I guess he had a lot of complexes," admitted Mike, "as people of small stature sometimes have. It wasn't easy being a short guy even then, but he was fast and cunning. He could outthink, outmaneuver and out-ad-lib almost everyone. He had inherited the blarney of great Irish poets like Sean O'Casey, and the quick fists and fighting skills of the great Irish-American boxers like Paddy Ryan and John L. Sullivan."

Mike's father blarneyed and battled his way through those very difficult years. He was quick and strong and wiry. Mike remembers the athletic skills his father possessed and the humiliating ways he would occasionally use them.

"Well, it's my birthday, boys. I guess you know that, or you wouldn't have sung the song, now would ya?"

"We all knew what was coming next," remembered Mike. "But there was nothing we could do about it. The cake, the presents, the birthday song were never enough.

"So, out in the streets with ya," he would say, "and we'll see how well you're doing against ole Daddy."

Michael and Robert dutifully followed their father out on the streets of Proviso township.

"Shall I be giving you a head start this year again, boys?" he taunted them. "Well then, off with ya."

And Mike and Robert would run as fast as they could run. Year after year they ran, and still their father beat them. Even at their prime he could hit a stickball or kick a football farther—or run a race faster—than either of them, and he never let them forget it. He was proud and tough and Irish, and he wanted his sons to be proud and tough and Irish. So, when Michael, Jr. decided at such a young age to be a singer, Michael, Sr. was not greatly pleased.

"My father didn't like the idea at all. He wanted me out there on the fields and in the vacant lots, playing baseball or football with my brother."

Mike was small, like his father, but built like an athlete. The coaches groaned when Mike refused to take sports seriously—he was short, but he could kick and throw with the best of them. Thirty years later Mike Douglas proved his prowess on nationwide television when he hit the stickball farther than both Johnny Bench and Micky Mantle. But already as a child he knew he wanted to sing, and was constantly preoccupied with his singing.

"Mom didn't want me to take sports seriously. She was afraid I was going to get hurt—break my nose or sprain my ankle—and ruin some big chance at a showbiz career that lay in my path just ahead. My brother Bob was always coming home with broken bones or sprained muscles. I was the strong one in our family. I was tough like my dad and I desperately wanted to please him, but I knew that one day I would be a singer on that Chicago Theatre stage, and every day I grew more preoccupied with making that dream come true. My dad watched me and seemed to grow more and more disappointed as he watched."

Michael Delaney Dowd, Sr. stood in the doorway of Rafferty's, a pint of bitters in his hand. Michael, Jr. walked up the street, schoolbooks in hand, and didn't see his father standing there. Suddenly, a small group of Italian boys surrounded Michael, Jr. to tease their Irish neighbor a bit. One of the boys pushed young Michael to the ground. Dowd, Sr. stood in the doorway watching, waiting for his son to strike. But Michael just picked up his books and walked through the crowd as though nothing had happened. It broke his father's heart to see a Dowd whacked by a scrawny neighbor kid and—worse—to see a Dowd walk away without whacking back.

Michael, Sr. charged out of that doorway with a roar of anger. The neighborhood boys disappeared wide-eyed in a cloud of dust. But it was Michael, Jr. he was after, not them. He grabbed his son by the shoulder and led him home.

"Michael," he said, his voice quivering, "you'll meet me in the garage at seven-thirty. Don't be late."

"My dad was a fierce disciplinarian," remembered Mike. "He had a wide belt—actually, it was an old leather razor strap—hanging in the garage. It was thick and scary and left red welts on bare bottoms. And when Dad felt we deserved that belt he would book the beating like an agent books an auditorium or a speaker a speaking event. It was awful to have a reservation for an early beating in the garage but, looking back, I can see Dad's appointments were probably a stroke of genius. Both of us had time to cool down before the punishment was administered. Both of us had time to understand each other's position in the interim. At any rate, whether we

thought it fair or unfair, it was Dad's way of making us tough
and helping us remember.

*"Michael, it's seven-thirty, and you know why you're going
to get whacked?"*
"No, Dad. I don't."
*"Because you let that kid knock you down and get away
with it, that's why."*
"But Dad, why should I . . ."
"Michael," interrupted his father, *"Never, ever let someone
whack you without whacking them back."*
*With that advice, Michael, Sr. took down the leather strap
and administered the only justice he knew to his younger son.*

"My dad wasn't cruel. He didn't punish me that day out
of uncontrolled anger, but because he truly believed that only
the tough survive. I believe he beat me that day because he
wanted me to make it. That's why he pushed me toward sports,
toward boxing and baseball and football. He wanted me to
grow up tough and competitive. He wanted me to win. That
next day I saw the kid who knocked me down on that same
street and I gave him what my dad would call an 'honorable
whacking.' "

Michael, Jr. tried to please his father. He played sports.
He won his share of honors on the field and vacant lots. And
he whacked his share of bullies on St. Bernadine-Grade-School
and Proviso-High-School playgrounds. But Michael, Sr. finally
saw that his younger son was hopelessly hooked on being a
singer. When he realized that a career in entertainment was
inevitable for Michael, he gave in. His favorite expression was,
"Be the best." And when he resigned himself to Mike's singing
career, he took his son aside one day and gave him valuable
advice.

"Michael," he asked, "where are you going to do all this
singing?"

"I'm going to do it here, Dad, in Chicago. I'll sing whenever
and wherever they'll let me."

Michael, Sr. looked down at his rough, working-man hands and then up to his son.

"No," he said finally. "Not in Chicago."

"Why, Dad," Michael asked. "It's the only place I know."

"If you're going to be in the big leagues, son," advised his father, "then go where the big leaguers play. Go to New York or to Los Angeles. That's where you'll make it, not here."

It was probably sound advice, although a little premature for a kid in junior high school. But even then, being second place was no honor for Michael, Sr. He wanted top honors for his kids and would be satisfied with nothing less. Mike remembers well the awful days when parents still signed report cards.

"I walked up to him, my report card in hand. I was proud of my marks, glad for the good news those numbers bore. He sat at the kitchen table slowly reading down the list of grades. The lowest grade on the card was a 97. He read down through all the 100s and spotted the 99 and then the 97. Then he looked up at me.

"Michael, why didn't you get all 100s?"

"At that point I felt like throwing in the towel. If those grades didn't please him, nothing would. I knew that I could never be good enough to satisfy him."

"Well," he asked again, "why aren't they all 100s?"

"That was a terrible mistake on his part. I can see it now, but Dad didn't have the benefits of Child Psychology 101 or of Dr. Spock and Ann Landers. He only knew that his son, Michael Delaney Dowd, Jr. should be number one. Nothing less would do."

"I tried hard, Dad," I mumbled, "I thought you would be happy with. . . ."

Then his father spotted the ranking number on Mike's card. In the class of forty-four at St. Bernadine's Grade School, the students were ranked in their grade standing. It was an awful system. Children who ranked low would be ridiculed on the playground—"Hello, number thirty-nine," or "There goes number thirty-three."

"What's this rank, number two, mean, Michael?" His father asked, pointing at the number and knowing full well what it meant.

"It means I'm the second-smartest person in my class," Mike answered proudly.

"Instead of smiling up at me, instead of taking me in his arms and holding me and telling me he loved me and was proud of my work, he said, 'Who is number one?' "

"The only kid ahead of me in the entire class was Tim O'Connor, another Irish boy who lived a few brownstones down the street from us. Dad knew their family. He and Tim's dad shared drinks occasionally at Rafferty's pub."

"You mean to tell me you let that O'Connor kid beat you? Michael, why aren't you number one? Next time show that O'Connor what a Dowd can do."

"And that was that," Mike recalled. "I don't know what those awful moments did to shape me. Perhaps I should be grateful. His words still echo in my brain. Perhaps his words made me tougher than his razor strap. Perhaps that's why I've survived in this business so long. Still, how I ached to hear him say, 'Well done, kid.' He never said it, then, when I needed it most. Later he tried, now and then, with a look or a gesture, and there were a few times when we made connection—when we were able to communicate the real love we had for each other. I remember how I felt when I heard about his reaction to a letter I wrote just before I went on active duty in World War II. . . ."

Michael Delaney Dowd, Jr. climbed down from the green military transport that had carried him from the arrival platform at Los Angeles's Grand Terminal.

"Welcome to Long Beach, sailor." The guard on duty saluted smartly and admitted Mike into the Long Beach Navy Port area.

"Name?" asked the young Navy lieutenant on duty at a desk nearby.

"Michael Delaney Dowd, Jr., Sir."

The lieutenant went through the pile of orders and found Mike's.

"S.S. Carole Lombard, sailor. Berth 3. Follow the yellow signs. You can't miss her."

"But you can try," chimed in a sailor standing nearby. Mike walked over to the stranger, shifted his duffle bag to the ground, and stood tearing open his orders.

"Why should I miss her?" he asked casually.

"Because she's an ammo ship," the stranger answered. "Ten thousand tons of ship and four thousand of them bombs, cannon shells, torpedoes, and other assorted fireworks."

Mike walked towards Berth 3. The little Liberty ship awaiting him would carry Mike to all three of the major war zones from Europe to Africa to Asia and back. . . .

". . . And with no escort, either," added a sailor standing beside him on the deck a little later in the day.

"You mean we'll be sailing this floating time-bomb around the world with no escorts?" Mike asked incredulously.

"That's right, buddy boy," answered his new friend. "Why would anybody escort us? One direct hit and we become the enemy. Everything for miles around would be torched by the stuff we're carrying and go down to Davy Jones beside us."

The loneliness of the first night aboard the QEII was nothing in comparison to the loneliness Mike felt the day the S.S. Carole Lombard sailed away from Long Beach Harbor. The last line was dropped. Tugs were nudging the Lombard towards the harbor entrance.

"Hey, neighbor," Mike yelled to a sailor on the dock. "Do me a favor and drop this in a mailbox, will you?"

Mike leaned far over the railing and barely got the envelope into the stranger's hand before the ship was moving rapidly towards the Pacific.

"Don't worry," yelled the stranger. "I'll mail it today."

Mike had spent all the night before writing to his dad, and he didn't want the Navy censors to read that letter.

"I suppose it sounds melodramatic now," Mike confessed. "But I didn't really think that I would be coming back. So I wrote my dad all those things you want to say in person but just can't do it somehow."

Mike told him about his fears of going to war on a tiny Liberty ship loaded with high explosives. He told him about the insurance policy he had taken out for Gen, and that his wife was moving back to live with her folks in Oklahoma while he was out to sea. He addressed the letter to his dad at work, hoping his mother would not see it and be worried by it.

"At the end of the letter I told my dad that I loved him and that if I didn't come home from the war he should always remember that I died loving him."

Mike had no idea how the letter would affect his father. Later he learned that Michael Delaney Dowd, Sr. wept when he read it and kept it in a locked box in the dresser by his bed. Michael, Sr. almost wore out that letter reading and re-reading it while his son crisscrossed the world carrying ammunition for the men and women fighting in all three theatres of the war.

Mike and the crew of the S.S. Carole Lombard sailed thirty-six days without seeing a strip of land. The Navy was taking no chances with that cargo, and so they gave Asia a wide berth and sailed wide around the Marshall Islands, Fiji and New Caledonia, down past Brisbane and the west coast of Australia, through the stormy Tasman sea, and finally into Perth on the southeast coast of Australia.

The QEII could make that same voyage smoothly. Her twin set of giant wing-like stabilizers could reduce the roll in rather severe weather to no more than three degrees. But the Carole Lombard had no stabilizers, and she bucked wildly in the fierce waves crashing across the Tasman Sea.

Crewmen lay on their bunks and groaned. Brave men turned white with fear and seasickness as giant waves loomed above the little ship.

"Time for dinner, fellows," Mike called out good-naturedly as he passed between the swinging hammocks.

He still doesn't know why seasickness never struck him. Neither did his friends on board, and they told him with no uncertain words what to do with his suggestion about eating.

"Dowd, are you actually eating again?" asked the cook when Mike entered the galley.

"Why not?" he answered, "I'm hungry."

By then he was alone in the ship's mess, with only one greenish-hued cook to keep him company. Even the ship's officers were struggling against that nauseous malady.

"We were doing thirty-degree rolls for about four days," Mike remembers. "You could see the waves towering above us and hear the ship crash, bow down, into the trough. Then she would shake and crawl up that wall of water again."

The mess hall tables had railings around their edges so the plates and cups could slide back and forth without falling to the deck. Mike learned to grab a bite when the plate was before him, chew while the plate lurched back across the table, then grab another bite upon the plate's return. For at least four days he ate almost alone.

There were bad days on that cruise, even in the calmer waters. For thirty-six days they rode the little ship sitting atop four thousand tons of highly explosive cargo. With the storms, the bad food, the cramped and crowded quarters—and no sight of land—the men "got a bit testy."

"We had been at sea too long," Mike explained, "and some of those merchant-marine types who sailed with us had been prohibited from other duty by their prison or bad conduct records. Fights broke out at regular intervals. In fact," he added, "the fighting got so bad that two guys could beat the socks off each other and nobody would even look up."

Finally, the captain mounted a ring out on the open deck. Men who wanted to fight squared off before the other sailors and, with a referee on hand, fought it out. But fights continued to erupt without warning all over the ship, and far from the constrained civilities of that boxing ring. It was during this cruise that Michael's training in toughness paid off.

"Hey, Dowd," yelled a sailor passing Mike's bunk. "What's that growing under your nose?"

Mike had grown a black handlebar mustache on the cruise. He had waxed, combed, and shaped it into a tonsorial wonder. It wasn't the first time he had been teased or called a pirate or a gigolo because of that splendid mustache.

Mike ignored the jibe and continued reading on his second-level bunk.

"I'll bet it's just pasted on," heckled the sailor again. "And I'll bet I can pull it off," he boasted.

"Be my guest," Mike answered, still not looking up.

The sailor reached out with both hands and grasped the mustache firmly, but even before he could pull at it Mike dropped his book and hit the taunting sailor in the face with such a Michael, Sr. whack that it split the sailor's lip and bloodied his nose. The man walked away, blood spurting, and Mike picked up his book and began to read again.

"I hate violence," Douglas remembered years later. "I was shocked to see what my fist did to that poor sailor's face. I suppose my dad would have been proud that this one time Michael, Jr. didn't let himself get pushed around. I spent so much of my life trying to please my father, and only once or twice can I remember his acknowledging that."

Fishing boats and pleasure cruisers lined both sides of the Baltimore harbor entrance. Flags waved. A Navy band played "Stars and Stripes Forever" on the pier. A huge sign welcomed back the S.S. Carole Lombard, its officers and crew. Hundreds of family members and friends crowded up to the restraining barriers on the pier. Newborn infants were held up for proud fathers to see. Sailors craned their necks for sight of wives and faithful sweethearts. Gen stood in the crowd, trying to pick out Mike in the blur of blue whirling, saluting, streaming down the gangplank.

Mike saluted the ensign and rushed down into the crowd.

"Mike, Mike! Over here!" Gen yelled at the top of her lungs. And Mike pushed through the crowd and into her waiting arms. For a moment in that warm, long-awaited embrace he closed his eyes to savor Gen in his arms again.

They took the transport train to Chicago, where another festive scene greeted them. Michael and Gen looked out over the sea of faces. And there, in the crowd, almost hidden from view, stood Michael Delaney Dowd, Sr.

Both men stood staring across the distance between them. Michael, Sr. stood with his hands at his side. Neither man knew exactly what to say or do next. Michael, Jr. was home. For him the horrible war had ended and he was alive and well. A million other fathers would greet the remains of their sons and daughters on that pier and piers like it around the world. So many boys and girls would not come back at all. And suddenly all the pride and toughness of that old Irishman gave in to the love and pride and gratitude he felt. He rushed across the space, grabbed Mike in his arms and for one brief moment held him tight.

"For just a split second he stood there hugging me," remembered Mike. "Then, just as suddenly, he realized what he was doing and pulled back. His arms let me go again and dropped like weights to his side."

"Welcome home, son," Mr. Dowd said gruffly. Then he took Mike's heavy duffle bag, swung it lightly onto his shoulders and led the way to the waiting car.

"It was very quick as hugs go," Mike recalled later, "but thirty-six years later I can still feel his arms around me and remember how very much it meant to have them there."

There are other ways Mike's dad proved how proud he was of his son's success. Often through the years, in Chicago, when he went to a store or garage and an attendant or clerk would ask, "May I help you?" Michael, Sr. would answer, "My son is Mike Douglas, you know." And immediately a conversation would begin with yet another fan of "The Mike Douglas Show." It was Michael, Sr.'s opening line so often that Mrs. Dowd got embarrassed by it, and Mike had to hire personnel just to send autographed pictures to bars and grocery stores and barbershops where Michael, Sr. had visited and promised an eager clerk or attendant something special "from my famous son."

But proud as he was of his son's success, Michael, Sr. was only rarely able to tell him so. Michael, Jr. spent a lifetime reaching out, but still can count on one hand the times he felt his father reaching back. Perhaps the last time is the easiest to remember.

Michael Delaney Dowd, Sr. lay in the antiseptic silence of his hospital room. The only sounds Michael, Jr. could hear were the quiet beeps from a bedside medical monitor and the tortured breathing of his father on the bed. A life-long smoker, Michael, Sr. was dying painfully of emphysema. Tubes protruded from his mouth and nose. Dark, unpleasant liquids flowed back and forth in the tubes. Phlegm rattled in the old man's chest. Death hovered nearby.

Mike stared down at his father from the end of the bed, his heart breaking with helplessness. He looked into those eyes— once so full of mischief and merriment—and saw them clouded, grey, and teary. Those once strong arms were now thin, flesh folding over flesh, and an intravenous needle, taped precariously, pulsed what life was left into him. That once-barrel chest heaved up and down for oxygen, and sheets draped thin, weak legs that once had raced and beaten his boys on birthdays past.

Finally, Mike moved to his father's side and whispered, "Dad, I love you." The old man looked confused. His hearing had failed. Mike shouted one last time. "Dad, I love you." Slowly his father turned and looked into Michael's eyes. Then, painfully, he nodded. Unable to speak, he was signaling across the distance that had separated them—"Son, I love you, too."

"It wasn't much," Mike remembers, "but it was enough."

It is a melancholy experience to walk the decks at night when other passengers are sleeping. Memories flow when one stands alone and feels the rhythm of the sea or watches moonlight sparkle its path across the water. Mom and Dad Dowd would not be there to greet Michael, Jr. when this transatlantic cruise ended. Both had died, yet he could still feel his mother's hand in his as the Jimmy Dorsey band played those many years past. He could still sense her excitement pouring into him when the trumpet fanfare sounded and the show began. He could still see his father standing in the doorway of Rafferty's Pub, a pint of stout in his hand and a fierce look of pride and Irish determination in his eyes. Somehow Mike was both of them. They were gone now, but what Mike Douglas is those two people had breathed into him with their lives.

For years, few people knew about the DeBolt family unless they'd seen them interviewed on "The Mike Douglas Show." Yet of all the celebrities I have met and interviewed, the DeBolts still haunt me for the beauty and the simplicity of their lives. In addition to their six biological children, there are thirteen others, Korean, Vietnamese and American-born, who are theirs by adoption or legal guardianship. Many of those kids are so emotionally or physically handicapped that no one besides the DeBolts would have them. They have given so much hope it amazes me. On the show, when they talk about their kids, their eyes fill up with tears of joy. What seems incredibly tough by normal standards has been a source of great reward for them."

MIKE DOUGLAS

We try to raise and train a child for early emancipation. We give our children love, but we are also demanding, and we believe in discipline. . . . We are not an institution for the handicapped. We don't want any child here for the rest of his or her life. We usually want every one of these disabled children to reach a point—just as our able-bodied children do—where he or she will come to us and say, "Mom and Dad, I think I am ready to leave the house and make it on my own." Before a child can make such a break, he must face the reality of himself and know how to deal with the reality around him. The world is not handicap-oriented. The handicapped must deal with the world of the able-bodied. They're going to have to make it and function as effective human beings in a system that is in no way geared to their crutches, braces, and blindness.

BOB DEBOLT

Chapter Three

GENEVIEVE PURNELL DOUGLAS thanked Lynn Faragalli, Mike's personal secretary, and Mike's valet for their help in unpacking and stowing the extensive Douglas traveling wardrobe. Mike would have to change his attire dozens of times during the next six days for the various television tapings, the gala events on board the QEII, the formal black tie dining in the Queen's Grill, as well as for jogging on the boat deck or working out in the gym.

Gen knew the pressure Mike and his crew were feeling. To tape full-hour entertainment shows in a Hollywood studio was one thing, but to produce them on a moving ship, thousands of miles out to sea and with absolutely no access to well-stocked television supply departments or the normal comforts and needs of the trade, made everyone, even Mike's seasoned professionals, a bit jumpy. Alone in the Trafalgar Suite, Gen bathed, changed into a dressing gown, and arranged the suite to be as comfortable and homelike as possible.

Downstairs, in the suite's giant living room, cast and crew were meeting. Upstairs, in their private quarters, Gen rearranged the vases of roses and carnations. She replaced the giant box of Cadbury chocolates provided by the Cunard Lines with Mike's box of Doublemint chewing gum, his favorite diet aid. And she placed silver-framed pictures of their three daughters and their families on the bureau where she and Mike could see and remember them.

Gen has a decorator's eye, and as she worked she glanced around appreciatively at the contents of the bedroom and the sitting room nearby. There were overstuffed chairs in floral patterns, a nautical bedspread and matching drapes, an antique brass ship's bell, an antique inlaid wooden writing table, and a beautiful full-scale model of Nelson's flagship, the Victory. And there were other nautical artifacts: a parallel rule by F. Wiggins and a polaris dial by T. B. Winter—both antique navigational devices used over a century and a half before— a Doulton ceramic stein, shaped like a pirate captain's head, for drinking stout, and several leather-bound, first-edition volumes describing Admiral Nelson and his naval conquests from the Nile to Trafalgar. On the center wall of the bedroom was a gold-framed portrait of Horatio Nelson and his epitaph by one of England's poet laureates, Robert Southey: "England has had many heroes. But never one who so entirely possessed the love of his fellow countrymen. All men knew that his heart was as humane as it was fearless . . . that with perfect and entire devotion he served his country with all his heart, and with all his soul, and with all his strength. And therefore they loved him as truly and fervently as he loved England."

Later that evening, as she waited in the sitting room for Mike to finish his meeting and come upstairs, Genevieve relaxed in one of those overstuffed chairs and reminisced about herself, Mike, and their life together.

"I have toured past that tall monument to Admiral Nelson in London's Trafalgar Square dozens of times during our visits to England," remembered Gen, "but it wasn't until tonight, thumbing through those beautiful old books on the table there, that I learned Trafalgar is the low, sandy cape on Spain's southern coast at the Western entrance to the Strait of Gibraltar, or that in 1805 Nelson's British fleet defeated the French and Spanish fleet fighting for Napoleon there, or that Nelson was fatally wounded during the battle."

Mike and Gen Douglas both love to read. In their Beverly

Hills home, rooms overflow with books in the process of or waiting to be read. During the almost twenty years of "The Mike Douglas Show," Mike and Gen read thousands of books and articles by and about their famous guests in order to interview them with intelligence and understanding.

"I suppose it was mother who passed on to me the love for words. My father, William Purnell, Sr., managed the shoe department in Oklahoma City's Sturms' Department Store. He was a devoted and loving father, a rather humble and loving man. But my mother was a firebrand. In fact, at 88 she still is a firebrand."

Gen recalled sitting beside her eighty-eight-year-old mother recently in the waiting room of a Los Angeles dentist's office.

"I'm not sure I want to go through with this," Mrs. Purnell *glanced uneasily at the waiting room door.*

"Mom, you must."

"Why? At my age you don't need teeth. You have plenty of time to gum your food to death."

The receptionist pushed back the sliding window that separated the waiting room from the business office.

"You may come in now Mrs. Purnell."

"I still think it's a waste of time," declared Mrs. Purnell as she entered the dentist's office and sat down in his chrome and plastic chair.

"Well, well," he said as he entered the room. "You win the prize, Mrs. Purnell. You're the oldest person I have ever had the pleasure to serve."

In spite of her quiet, mumbled resistance, over the next thirty minutes the doctor removed two of her teeth, leaving intermittently to see other patients in other rooms.

"You know, doctor," Mrs. Purnell said when the doctor was finally through. "You sure are pretty. Good looking, too. But I think you owe it to your patients to work on one person at a time instead of wandering in and out so. It gives us patients too much time to think about the next horror you have up your sleeve."

"My mother has never been afraid to comment on anything to anybody," Gen recalled. "When I was in grade school in Oklahoma City, she had already become a kind of legend in her day. She was president of the P.T.A., a founder of the Women's Christian Temperance Union in Oklahoma City, and an energizing force in her women's political club, the Jeffersonians. She was elected Oklahoma City's most valuable citizen one year for her contribution in time and energy to so many important causes."

Genevieve Douglas still shows proudly the scrapbook of her mother's achievements as one of the few women then who were unafraid to take on the rough-and-tumble world of politics. Her mother spent many evenings at meetings across the city and around the state. She managed the election campaigns for local and statewide officeholders, including one Oklahoma governor, and wrote speeches for important political figures as well as writing the civic-club and political-organization addresses she delivered herself.

"Still," said Gen, "the children of parents who are actively involved in changing the world must pay some price for their parents' involvement. I was no exception."

The sixth grade history class had ended at Oklahoma City's Jefferson Grammar School. All the test papers had been returned but one. The bell rang and students headed for their lockers.

"Could I see you just a moment, Genevieve?" the teacher asked quietly from her desk.

Gen picked up her textbook and walked slowly to face Miss Jackson.

"Gen, what happened? Your test on the Constitution didn't turn out well at all."

Gen looked away, not knowing what to say and feeling awkward and embarrassed. After all, if anybody should understand government it would be the daughter of a parent who managed statewide election campaigns.

"Gen, you've done much better work than this before. What's happening now? Are you studying at home?"

"I'm having trouble with this unit, Miss Jackson."

"Well, ask your mom to help," answered the teacher. "She knows this material firsthand."

"I can't ask her to help, right now," answered Gen. "She's out politicking."

Suddenly, the teacher put down the paper and began to laugh.

"Out politicking, is she? Well, good for her. Don't worry about this test, Gen. I'll give you some extra help after class. I certainly wouldn't want your mom to let us women down out there in that man's world, would you?"

The teacher smiled at Gen, and they walked arm in arm from the classroom together.

Gen's mom had two sisters who also served as strong role models in Gen's life. Her mother's sister, Christine, was a dress designer in Oklahoma City with her own salon in Kerr's fashionable department store. Christine's set the city's pace for women's fashions and Genevieve, even as a young girl, loved to visit her aunt's showroom, to feel the fabrics and drape them on her arms or shoulders.

"Come here, Genevieve," called Aunt Christine from across the showroom. "I want you to help me decide."

Gen hurried past the racks of designer dresses and the tailors fitting the rather grand clientele who patronized Christine's.

"Tell me, young lady," said her aunt, "Which of these two colors goes best with your brown hair and blue eyes?"

Gen took the fabrics in her hands. She draped the powder-blue silk over one arm and the deep-brown satin over the other. She walked to the floor-length mirror and held up first one fabric, then the other.

"I think the blue," said Gen, a little uncertain because they were both very beautiful.

"Why the blue, Gen? Tell me why."

"It's just a feeling."

"That isn't enough. Tell me why you have that feeling.

You have made an excellent choice, but you must know why."

Gen held up the blue on one arm and let her long chestnut-colored hair spill down across it.

"The blue goes so well. They're different yet they—they seem to help each other, my eyes, and my complexion."

"Well said," replied her aunt, smiling. "But why not the brown?"

For a moment Gen stared at her reflection in the mirror. "The brown is beautiful and feels so rich, but it seems too much like the color of my hair and yet not the same."

"Exactly," praised her aunt. "The brown in your hair competes with that brown satin shade while the blue complements and sets off your hair and eyes. Good choice, Gen. Let's have lunch."

Gen loved to go with her Aunt Christine to her apartment in the nearby Skirvin Hotel. Christine lived in a hotel apartment with her mother, Grandma Richards. Gen's maternal grandparents had moved to Oklahoma during the oil rush at the beginning of this century. But Grampa Richard's wells had turned out to be dry. He had lost everything in those heady, high-risk days when billions were won or lost on a gamble. After his bankruptcy had come World War I. One of the Richardses' seven children, LaGrand, a teenager, had begged permission to enter the service, though he was one year too young to enlist. Grampa Richards had refused. But Hattie Mae Richards, Gen's grandma, under heavy coaxing from her much-loved son, had finally signed the enlistment papers. Grampa Richards had never forgiven his wife, and eventually they had divorced. He had moved to Long Beach, California, to open a business of his own there and died.

So Grandma Hattie Mae Richards had gone to work supporting her children. Her industrious and daring style was passed on to her daughters—Gen's mother, Gen's Aunt Christine, and her Aunt Margene. The third daughter married the owner of a large flour mill in Yukon, Oklahoma, and wrote a cookbook for baked goods featuring Oklahoma honey biscuits and cloverleaf rolls. Gen described those family reunions at Aunt Margene's where the tables were spread with turkey and giblet dressing, with hams cooked in pineapple and honey, with hot biscuits dripping in fresh butter, with poke greens and apple pie and fresh peach ice cream.

"We certainly weren't rich," remembered Gen, "but we had everything a family could ask for. Our little Oklahoma City house echoed with music. My brothers played drums and rhythm instruments, my mom played the piano, and the whole family sang at the top of our lungs."

She remembers one musical session with less fondness.

Gen threw her school books down on the desk in her room, kicked off her shoes and sprawled on her bed. It had been a hard day at school, and she needed time to relax and think. Arms folded behind her head, she stared around the room idly. In the parlor, her brother, Charles, put a punched roll into the player piano, and the familiar sounds of "The Band Played On" interrupted the silence.

"Turn it off, Charles," she yelled.

The music continued, only a strange and primitive percussion sound picked up the beat.

"O.K., Charles, leave on the piano but cut the drumming, please!" Gen called again with no results.

She groaned and rolled over and reached for a pillow to cover up her head when she noticed that the shelf above her bed was empty. Her entire doll collection was missing. Surely, that awful drumming sound coming from the parlor couldn't be. . . .

Gen rolled off her bed and ran into the parlor screaming.

"Charlie, did you take my dolls?"

She stopped in horror, for there, held in place by a double row of old books, were her dolls, all propped up in place with Charlie beating out a rhythm on their heads.

"Their eyes were bugging out. Their heads were cracking open. It was an awful sight," remembers Gen.

"Charlie," she yelled, rushing him full force. "Stop it!"

Books fell. Dolls collapsed. Gen and her brother wrestled to the floor.

"We used to get in spats," said Gen, "but Charles was also the kind of brother who liked me to dress up so that he could take me out and show his buddies what a 'beautiful sis' he had. We had so much fun together, the three of us. My brothers' buddies were always at the house. I guess I was really around more boys than girls in my childhood. I've always felt comfortable around men. I was 'one of the boys' in my neighborhood. I climbed trees and hung by my legs and ate apples upside down."

On Saturdays, Gen and her brothers and their friends lined up for the motion picture matinees and watched the same features and serials that Michael Delaney Dowd, Jr. and his mother were watching in Chicago. After the films Gen and her brothers and their friends would act out the story again. They built stagecoaches for the Western dramas and cardboard tanks for the war movie plots.

"I was barely out of the tree-climbing stage when I met Mike," Gen confessed. "Radio Station WKY was in the Skirvin Hotel where my Aunt Christine and Grandma Richards had their apartment. I was seventeen. Mike was eighteen. And we often passed each other in the hall or the elevator of the Hotel. Our parents and friends didn't know about our marriage, so for those first few weeks of married life it was about the only way we saw each other. Then Mike was ordered to boot camp at the Great Lakes Naval Academy, and before we had really gotten together to celebrate our wedding we were separated again."

The QEII steamed silently around the southern coast of England and into the waters of the Atlantic. Gen leaned back in her chair and sighed deeply. The day had been exhausting: packing in London, one more press conference at the Ritz, the long drive to Southampton, more television interviews while boarding the QEII, and the unpacking and moving into the Trafalgar Suite for their North Atlantic crossing.

But Gen was an experienced traveler. Almost from the beginning of her life with Mike, she had been on the road. Together they had traveled thousands of hours and hundreds of thousands of miles by car, bus, train, taxi, limousine, small private planes, jumbo jets—even the Concorde. Her life had been lived at almost supersonic speed, and all because Genevieve Purnell Dowd Douglas had determined early in their married life that she would not be separated for very long intervals from the man she loved. If at all possible, she would be there beside him, wherever his career might lead. She would do her best to transform a rented room in the attic of an old Chicago brownstone or the grand penthouse suite of the QEII into another home away from home. And every night of their married life she would try her best to be there waiting up for him if it meant packing and unpacking a million times or more.

"Being together is at the heart of making a marriage work," she claimed. "It is just too easy to go off in two different directions and find that in the distance you have grown apart, love is lost forever."

Gen was only a teenager when she decided that separation could destroy a marriage faster than anything. Mike was in boot camp at the Great Lakes Training Station near Chicago. Gen was still living in Oklahoma City with her parents. Neither the Purnells nor the Dowds knew that their two children had been married by a justice of the peace in Norman, Oklahoma. Mike and Gen wrote each other almost every day, but it was not enough. Gen grew anxious. Mike felt lonely and cut off. Even though they were each near their families, Mike and Gen needed to be together. So Gen took a job in the little gift shop, and she saved every dime she made to buy a one-way ticket to Chicago.

"Daddy, I'm ready," seventeen-year-old Gen said nervously.

Her father looked up to see his only daughter standing at the kitchen door.

"I hope you don't mind my using your old suitcase," she

*said, looking down at the brown, heavy cardboard case with
its thin metal corners and its wide leather handle. Then she
looked up at him again. Gen was wearing that same blue Sunday
suit with its white neck and collar. Pinned firmly in her hair
was a small white straw hat. He could see that she was blinking
back the tears.*

*For the first time William Purnell, Sr. saw the woman stand-
ing where his little girl used to stand. For the first time he
felt that awful ache a parent feels when he discovers that his
daughter will not be his little girl forever.*

*Mrs. Purnell entered the kitchen and saw her husband staring
at young Gen. Now there were tears in his eyes too. He looked
from his daughter to his wife with a kind of quiet desperation.*

"Why, Dad," she said. "I do believe you are crying."

*Mr. Purnell wiped awkwardly at his tear-brimmed eyes with
his handkerchief.*

*"She's only going to visit Mike," she reminded her husband.
"And she'll be living with the Dowds and be perfectly well chaper-
oned by them. Won't you, Gen?"*

*Gen nodded, then quickly turned away. Her eyes were filled
with tears. Her palms felt cold and sweaty. Why couldn't she
tell them? This would not be a short-term visit. This was a
final good-bye, the good-bye a son or daughter speaks when
he or she takes that first step away from home and family
into someone else's life forever.*

*They stood there in the kitchen door, tears flowing freely
now. Dad tried to squeeze his daughter tight and bumped her
little hat in the process. Mom Purnell pinned it back in place
again.*

*"Good-bye, darling," she said. "Have a wonderful visit. Mike
is a good boy. Tell him that we love him, won't you?"*

*Gen lugged her daddy's old suitcase out to the car, waved
one last good-bye, and then set out to follow the man she would
spend her life following.*

"So I went to the big city," remembered Gen. "The Dowds
lived in a Chicago flat. I didn't even know what a flat was.

Oklahoma City had few high-rise buildings then, no crowded slums, no ethnic neighborhoods. The Dowd family flat had only two bedrooms and very little extra space, but what space they had they shared with me. During the week I walked down the streets of Chicago or along the Lake. I felt the changing moods of that great city. I loved the cacaphony of sounds and smells and sights that echo up from the Greek and the Latin, the Chinese and the Italian sections. I walked and waited for those twenty-four-hour leaves when Mike would run up all three flights of stairs and hold me in his arms again."

It was Monday. Mike had just returned to base. Genevieve sat in the Dowd flat with a fresh pad of white stationery and matching envelopes she had purchased at the corner drug store.

"Dear Mom and Dad. . . ."

Actually, during her time with the Dowds she had written often. But her folks were getting anxious for her return. She had to tell them about their marriage. But every time she tried, the attempt got wadded up and tossed into the growing pile of paper in the wastebasket at her feet.

"On April 6, Mike and I were married. . . ."

What would her mother think? Would she resent them? Gen was Mrs. Purnell's only daughter. There would be no church wedding, no list of special friends, no showers or cakes or pictures in white lacy dresses. How would Dad Purnell feel? He couldn't stand in a rented tux and answer the minister's "Who gives this woman?" with his own brave "Her mother and I do."

"We are very much in love. . . ."

But was love an excuse to disobey her parents, to lie to them, to the justice of the peace, to forge those changes on their marriage license? Was love a good enough reason to jump into a lifetime commitment hardly knowing each other, never even having dated?

"You're not losing a daughter; you're gaining a son. . . ."

It was an old line, even then. But it was true. Both her parents knew and loved Mike. But they also knew Mike was just a kid in the service and Gen their only daughter—still in high school. *Would they worry that the marriage wouldn't last, that Gen and Mike's love would not be forever? Or would they give their blessing?*

"I didn't need to worry," remembered Gen. "My parents wrote back immediately, congratulating us and wishing us the very best. 'We knew you two kids were in love,' they wrote, 'and we know your love will last forever.'

"And it has," said Gen gratefully, leaning forward to emphasize her point. "And one of the very chief reasons it has lasted," she affirmed, "is that we refuse to be separated very long or very often."

When Mike was transferred from the Great Lakes Naval Center to the University of Wisconsin's training program in communications for Navy officer candidates, she followed him again. She was still only seventeen. There were no family members in Wisconsin, no family home or flat, but she had determined to stay with him wherever he went, whatever the cost. And stay with him she did!

"ROOM FOR RENT." The sign was posted on the porch of an old, two-story wooden home near the extension center of the University of Wisconsin campus in Madison.

"Let's try it, Gen," Mike said enthusiastically. "The street is quiet and safe. The trees and the lawns are green. And it's only blocks from the base."

Hand in hand they walked up the stairs to ring the bell. An old woman led them slowly up the inside stairs of her home and into a very small room with a window looking out over the front-yard fence.

It was very sparse. A bed, one chest of drawers, an old lamp on a tall lamp stand, a tiny writing desk and a wardrobe. No closet. No private bath. Just a room to rent.

"How much?" asked Mike bluntly.

"Twenty-five dollars a month, with the first and the last month's rent paid in advance," the woman answered, looking away.

Mike groaned. "Twenty-five dollars a month?" It seemed like such a huge chunk of their meager income. But after a minute Mike said, "We'll take it, and Gen looked up at him with surprise. The room was so little and cost so much!

"You are married, aren't you?" said the lady, looking across the room suspiciously at Gen.

"Yes, we are," said Mike, whipping out the license they had altered together.

The woman took Mike's five ten-dollar bills, gave him the key to the room, and disappeared. Mike turned to Gen and held out the key.

"Welcome home, Mrs. Michael Delaney Dowd, Jr."

Then he took her in his arms, and they both began to laugh and cry together.

Mike was only home on weekends and on an occasional twenty-four-hour pass when he could arrange it. On the base an enterprising officer noticed that Mike had been a singer. He asked Mike to perform at the officers' club and for special events on the base. Mike was studying calculus, navigation, math, communication theory—even learning Morse code. And the singing dates kept him busy almost every evening. Sometimes during the week, after singing at the officers' club, Mike would sneak away from his quarters on the base just to kiss Genevieve goodnight before sneaking back onto the base again.

Gen lay alone in their tiny room, staring up at the ceiling. It was Monday morning. Mike had already gone back to the base for the week. She looked around her, taking in the cracked ceiling, the bare walls, and the second-hand furniture of their first home. She was half a nation away from her friends and family, in a strange city, living in a room without a refrigerator or a stove or a private bath. And she was feeling cold and lonely and homesick.

"Welcome home, Mrs. Dowd," Mike had said. Now it was up to her to transform that miserable room into a real home.

But they had almost no money left after that first big rental payment, and Mike's militay pay would hardly cover the necessities.

Gen Dowd jumped out of bed, showered in that communal bath, dressed, and began her first walk through Madison. In the distance, the dome of the white, granite state capitol reflected the sunshine off the lake nearby. (Madison, she soon discovered, was built on a narrow isthmus between Lakes Monona and Mendota.) She walked along the lake and past the stores on the commercial blocks around the capitol building. In one window, she noticed a "CLERK WANTED" sign, and walked in. With her experience in merchandising gained from years of working with her Aunt Christine at Kerr's Department Store in Oklahoma City, young Gen was soon appointed assistant manager of the Darling Dress Shop.

With her first paycheck, Gen bought colorful sheet material to make new drapes for their apartment window. She bought a vase for freshly picked flowers, and a red wooden Swedish candleholder with a beautiful white taper candle to burn in their window. Soon their room glowed with warm colors and fresh paint, and smelled of flowers and scented candles.

"Give me candles, flowers, and warm, friendly colors," she would say years later, "and I can make a home out of any room. Anybody can if she tries."

Gen ate one meal a day at the little cafe nearby. She also remembered buying dozens of boxes of chocolate-covered graham cracker cookies "to get me through the day, with pints and pints of milk to wash them down."

"I couldn't eat three meals a day in that cafe," she explained. "We didn't have that kind of money. So I just kept filling up on junk food and milk. I was young. I didn't realize my body wouldn't last forever. So I snacked for breakfast, snacked for lunch, then ate one meal at the diner nearby. It's a good thing we didn't live in Madison very long," she added. "I'm afraid I would have ended up looking very much like the Goodyear blimp."

In six months Mike was transferred to Long Beach Harbor. For the third time in less than a year, Gen packed her daddy's old suitcase and followed him, this time to California. At that moment, in Britain, three million allied troops were assembling for the D-Day invasion and reclamation of Axis-held Europe. The war in the Pacific had turned around, with U.S. troops taking the little-known but key Pacific Islands of Kwajalein, Truk, and Saipan. B-29 Superfortress bombers were fire-bombing cities in Japan, and the U.S. Pacific Fleet was maneuvering to face the Japanese fleet in the crucial battle for the Leyte Gulf.

America's westbound trains were crowded with servicemen and women heading for the West Coast debarkation ports to replace their war-weary counterparts on duty in the Pacific. Soldiers, sailors, airmen, and marines overflowed trains crossing the continental United States. Coaches groaned as they lurched down the tracks carrying five times the number of passengers they were built to carry. And only days after Mike left Madison on one of those trains en route to Long Beach, eighteen-year-old Gen climbed onto another crowded troop train to follow him.

"That trip was unbelievable," she recalled. "Men were sleeping on every chair, in the luggage racks, and on the floors of every compartment. The toilets and dining areas couldn't handle the extra passengers, so at every station a thousand men and I raced across the platform to the toilet and food lines forming. We were like a wave sweeping in and over the station, then ebbing back onto the train again."

Mike found a second room to rent in a private home, this time in downtown Los Angeles. East L.A. was even then a very ethnic neighborhood where far more Spanish than English was spoken. The people were poor and often unemployed. The area was rough and run-down and far from Mike's base in Long Beach. But it was all they could afford, and they had decided to stay together whatever it cost them in money or inconvenience.

Seldom did Mike and Gen have extra money for a date,

but two weeks before his sea duty orders arrived, the still newlyweds treated themselves to a movie at the Wilshire Theater on Wilshire Boulevard near their apartment.

"We sat in the theater trying to hold hands and eat popcorn at the same time during the feature," laughed Gen. "It was *Meet Me in St. Louis,* and it starred July Garland and the child actress Margaret O'Brian. Mike said that watching that little girl dance and sing that night made him wish we had daughters of our own."

"We hardly saw the newsreel that followed," added Gen, "after that wonderful, schmaltzy family musical. The Movietone News had a short feature on Clark Gable, who was christening a Liberty Ship at the Kaiser Steel Works. That ship was the S.S. Carole Lombard.

"I had only begun to get my candles and my flowers and my colored drapes into our apartment in East Los Angeles when Mike was assigned communications officer on that same ship and sent to sea."

Gen Dowd stood alone in the cavernous train terminal in downtown Los Angeles. For the fourth time in months she had packed her daddy's suitcase and gone on the road. Each time Gen had followed Mike, refusing to let anything separate them for long. This time she had no choice. Mike was sailing on that little ammunition ship into the war-wracked waters of the Pacific. There was nothing left to do but pack her candles and her clothes and head back home to Oklahoma City to wait for his return.

"Even in those crowded months as we moved from Oklahoma City to Chicago, from Chicago to Madison, and from Madison to Los Angeles we were building our marriage, strengthening our relationship by just being together," said Gen Douglas. "I was only a teenager, but I felt secure in knowing that Mike really loved me and I really loved him. When we were together we were passionate about everything, making love or making drapes, in each other's arms or in each other's hair. We talked about everything. We tried to reach a consensus on every decision instead of holding out for one side or the other. And when we were apart, even for a day, we wrote or called each other faithfully.

"There is no way to keep a love alive, whether in marriage or in friendship, unless two people care enough to remain in close, loving contact. It wasn't easy during the war years to manage that. It isn't easy now. But where Mike went, I went, and where Mike goes now, I go. I believe," said Gen, "that staying together is the secret of our almost forty years of marriage."

Gen Douglas was waiting up for Mike in the sitting room of the Trafalgar Suite when he came up from his first difficult conference with cast and crew and his lonely walk on deck. He looked around the room. The family pictures were in place. There were flowers on the bedside table. Gen sat in one of the comfortable chairs, reading the ship's daily newspaper. She looked up and smiled.

"Hi, Darling. How did it go?" she asked him.

Mike stood in the cabin's doorway. He remembered his seventeen-year-old bride standing outside the main gate of the Great Lakes Naval Center, or watching for him from that second-floor window of that one plain room in Madison, or running into his arms when he finally sailed home from sea duty on the S.S. Carole Lombard. He remembered how many times she had packed and unpacked, painted walls, sewn drapes, arranged flowers, and lit scented candles so that he would have a home to come home to. He remembered her in that blue Sunday suit, suitcase in hand, at station after station. And he smiled back. "Everything went fine, Gen," he said. "Everything went fine."

To be interviewed on a network show like mine can be tough.
The subject is no longer protected by his agent, his press
department, his entourage. He or she is alone before millions
of viewers. . . . Under those hot lights you can learn a lot about
a celebrity. They may have achieved greatness . . . in their field,
but they still feel insecure, defensive, and protective of the image
they have so carefully cultivated. Others are comfortable, open,
and honest under the toughest questioning. Carol Burnett is a
perfect example of the latter. She doesn't worry about being
upstaged. . . . She never goes for a cheap laugh at somebody
else's expense. She refuses to overshadow others or make anyone
feel uncomfortable in any way. I think the difference is that
Carol knows she is a comic genius. She has worked hard to
perfect her craft. . . . She knows who she is and what she can
do and has lost her fear that maybe it is all an illusion.

MIKE DOUGLAS

An image that you have of yourself will come to pass, good
or bad. The more you feed into your subconscious . . . "Why
do things always happen to me?" . . . those are the people
who are always breaking their legs; their car conks out. That's
the loser syndrome. . . . Make no mistake. I enjoy my success.
I do a whole number on myself when I walk down the hall
at C.B.S. "Miss Burnett's office"—Oh, is that a hoot! . . .
But I've worked for it all. . . . Occasionally I get a little mad
when someone comes up and says, "Well, you lucky stiff."
It's true I'm not poor any more. That's great. But I didn't
inherit it; it wasn't left on my doorstep. The opportunities are
there for all of us."

CAROL BURNETT

Chapter Four

THERE ARE TWO NIGHT CLUBS, five bars, and a gambling casino on the QEII. Night-owl passengers may drink and dance till dawn. There are two live trios, two large bands, a discotheque, soloists, dancers—even a hypnotist—to entertain the late night crowd who, in turn, consume a mountain of mixed nuts and pretzels washed down by a river of booze. In the aft section of that great ship, tucked quietly away from the frenzy of the disco dancers nearby, is the Double Down Bar. Mike Douglas sat at an almost hidden table, drinking a Coke and munching an occasional peanut, reminiscing about his many years "on the saloon circuit."

"It may sound strange, coming from a man who doesn't touch the stuff," he said, "but my first twenty years in show business were spent singing in nightspots like this one. In fact, my very first singing job was in a saloon."

Friday night at Rafferty's Pub was wondrously raucous. Chicago Irish gathered to drink stout, smoke strong cigars, swap tales of Belfast and the IRA, and sing songs of Killarney, Ring of Kerry, and Galway Bay. The pub was dense with smoke and reeked pleasantly of beer and grilled bangers. From a rough wooden platform the piano player man presided over the festivities with his heavy Irish brogue and his less-than-subtle stories and songs of Mother Ireland.

Michael Delaney Dowd, Jr. stood on the sidewalk fronting Rafferty's and peeked cautiously inside. Loren had entered bravely and stopped near the piano man to gesture Michael in.

"Come on, Michael," Loren whispered loudly. "It's his break. Get in here!"

The piano man limped down off the stool, a pint of Watney's ale in hand, and stood joshing with a few cronies watching the game of darts nearby.

Ten-year-old Michael Dowd wandered across the room, trying desperately to look as though he belonged there. No one noticed the little boys arguing near the stage.

"Get up there and sing, Michael."

"Sing what?" young Dowd answered, knowing their plan but pretending to forget it.

" 'Danny Boy,' you dummy, sing it now or he'll come back and we'll lose our chance."

Michael Delaney Dowd, Jr. climbed up on the makeshift stage, looked out at that room full of loud Irish men and rosy-cheeked Irish women, took a deep breath, and began to sing.

"O Danny boy, the pipes, the pipes are calling. . . ."

First one pub patron, then another, looked up and grew silent.

". . . From glen to glen, and down the mountainside. . . ."

"Listen to the wee lad. He's a singer, Gawd bless him."

". . . The summer's gone, and all the roses falling. . . ."

"Isn't that Dowd's lad, Michael?"

". . . It's you, it's you must go and I must bide."

Just as the song was ending, Loren threw a quarter that rolled noisily across the open stage and clunked as it fell against the wall. The room suddenly erupted in applause, and more quarters, along with dimes and nickels, tinkled at Michael's feet.

Quickly Loren gathered up the booty and headed for the door. Michael stood watching the crowd, that wonderful sound of cheers and applause still ringing in his ears.

"Come on, Michael. Let's get out of here before your dad shows up and gives us both a whacking."

"It was my first real money earned as a singer," recalled Mike Douglas. "There was over nine dollars in that pile full of change, and I was counting my half on the bed that night when my mother entered the room and saw the loot.

"So, Michael, you're rich, are you?"

"No, Mom," Michael answered. "Just a few dollars I earned with Loren today."

"And tell me, lad, how did you earn so much?"

"Singing," Michael answered, already feeling that razor strap on his bottom.

"And where were you singing for money, pray tell?"

"At Raf—" The name of the pub got stuck in his throat. His mother hated the place. Too many times she had entered it in search of her husband, hoping to find him before the week's pay had been drunk or gambled away.

"At Rafferty's, Mom," he finally answered.

"At Rafferty's Pub?" she asked.

"Yes, Mom. You see, Loren and I. . . ."

"And Loren, too, was singing at Rafferty's?" she interrupted.

"No, Mom, Loren threw the quarter to get the money started. And then everybody was throwing quarters and dimes and nickels. Look, Mom, four dollars and eighty-five cents, just from singing one song."

Mrs. Dowd stood staring at her son. She wanted him to be a singer. She had worked hard to train him for the stage— but not for Rafferty's! She sat down on the bed beside him.

"Did you sing well, Michael?"

"Yes, Mom."

"Did you earn the money?"

"Yes, Mom!"

"Then you may keep it," she said. "But you may not sing at Rafferty's again. I don't want my son singing in saloons— not yet, anyway."

"I learned later about saloon life and why my mother feared it. But even then she knew the saloon circuit might be the only place I could start my singing career."

"When I was sixteen I joined a local band, the Bill Carlsen Band of a Million Thrills. Most of the band members had been recruited from my neighborhood in Chicago. We traveled throughout the Midwest, singing in bars or at private parties— even a supermarket opening or two. Most of the men were in their late twenties. I was Mickey Dowd—an open-mouthed teenager learning about being on the road and the price one paid to be there."

The Mississippi River wound its way lazily through Dubuque, in southern Iowa. Between the river and the tracks of the Chicago, Milwaukee, and St. Paul railroad, which dissected the town, stood a large motel/restaurant complex that served the traveling salesmen, cattle-and-hog buyers, and occasional tourists who happened by. A neon sign flashed above the riverside resort, announcing the weekend appearance of "Bill Carlsen and His Band of a Million Thrills." The garish yellow sign could be seen by travelers going both north and south on State Highway 61.

The town's three taxis ferried band members from Dubuque's train depot to the motel that evening. Instruments were still being unloaded and music stands being set in place five minutes before their eight o'clock show was to begin. The crowd was noisy and paid no attention to Bill Carlsen when he mounted the stage, took up his baton, and gave the downbeat. The band tried to play over the noisy crowd to gets its attention, but the local conventioners and salesmen wouldn't be subdued.

"Shut up, you hicks!" the young piano player shouted from the bandstand. "Shut up and listen!"

Bill Carlsen looked across the band at his pianist and signaled him to be silent, but the piano player just kept shouting.

"Bunch of Iowa corn pones wouldn't know music if they stepped on it!"

The crowd heard the insults coming from the band's direction and responded in kind.

"You call that music? Sounds like a hog-calling contest."

The crowd laughed and joined in the banter.

"Somebody get Bob off stage," Bill Carlsen said to the band. Mickey Dowd and the drummer jumped to remove their friend from the piano bench and safely out of the room before real trouble broke out.

"Our piano player was usually drunk by sunset," Mike remembered. "We had to carry him to his room that night and leave him half-conscious on the bed."

Being on the road causes pain—the pain of long separations from wives and family, the pain of one-night relationships that end with the departure of the train, the pain of people who feel lonely and isolated and scared.

"And so they drank," Mike recalled, "and they smoked marijuana before it was 'in.' Today they may snort cocaine and shoot up with heroin, or still just drink too much and overdose on pills to get them going and pills to get them calmed again. I've seen it all since I was a kid in knee pants, and the results are always the same. One false high leads to another. The release from pain takes more and more to achieve until nothing does it anymore. Good lives end up wasted. Great talent is destroyed and lost forever."

Bill Carlsen stood before the noisy dining room, apologized for his piano player's rude remarks, and then introduced "Mickey Dowd to please the crowd." Mike sang an Irish ballad and the crowd settled. Then he sang, "When Irish Eyes Are Smiling" and the audience, though still stung by the barbs, applauded more than politely. By the time Mike sang, "Danny Boy," the crowd was clapping and stomping and hollering for more.

When the show ended, Michael watched Bill Carlsen walk into the piano player's room.

"You're through, Bob. Here's your ticket home."

Carlsen was a gentle man, but time and time again he had warned the man to keep the bottle corked. And time and time again Bob had appeared on stage too drunk to play. Michael

*helped the piano player to the station that night and onto the
last Chicago-bound train.*

"I've seen so many bright young talents ruined by drinking
and by drugs," said Mike. "That's one reason why I never
take a drink stronger than a Coca Cola or a pill more powerful
than an aspirin. Still, it was the saloon crowd that kept me
singing and paid my bills for my first twenty years in show
business."

Years later, during one of Mike's twenty-four hour Navy
leaves (Gen was still living with her folks in Oklahoma City),
Mike and his friend George Mather took a bus into Hollywood
to Earl Carroll's Theater Restaurant.

"It was a fancy saloon," Mike remembered as he sat in
the Double Down Bar. "The Cokes cost as much as the mixed
drinks because there was a non-stop floor show with a big
band, singers, dancers, and comedians for the intermission
standup routines to keep the patrons entertained and drinking."

*Mike listened to the singer on the stage. He was belting out
a rousing version of "When Johnny Comes Marching Home,"
and the dancers in silky stars and stripes were high-stepping
arm in arm into the fireworks finale. When the number ended,
Earl Carroll himself came on stage to introduce the next number.*

*"We have a real Johnny home from the war right here tonight.
His buddy told me backstage that this sailor has an Irish tenor
that just won't stop."*

*Mike Dowd looked up from his Coke with a strange feeling
that he was about to hear his own name mentioned from that
stage.*

*"Ladies and Gentlemen join me in a surprise welcome for
Mr. Michael Delaney Dowd. Come on up, sailor boy, and sing
for us."*

*The crowd cheered. The dancers gathered on stage around
the piano, and Michael Dowd walked up to the stage with a
lump in his throat as big as a basketball.*

He told the man at the piano to play "Danny Boy" in the key of C, and the pianist passed it on to the band. Suddenly Michael found himself on stage in one of Hollywood's most prestigious night spots, singing his Irish theme song with all the gusto he could muster. When the song ended, the audience was on its feet applauding. Earl Carroll took Mike and his buddy to their table and said, "Kid, when you get out of the Navy see me. You'll have a job waiting."

Two years later Mike and Gen drove from Oklahoma City to Los Angeles to cash in on that promised job. He had turned down an offer from WKY in Oklahoma City to pick up his old radio singing spot there, and the two freshly reunited teenagers headed back across the country to begin his career.

"I got an agent," remembered Mike. "Everybody said you have to get an agent, so I got one. Everett Crosby was Bing Crosby's brother. He marched into Earl Carroll's office demanding $300 a week 'for that sailor boy who sings.' Carroll had $125 to offer and wouldn't pay a penny more. So I got an agent but I lost the job."

Those were difficult days. Hollywood streets were crowded with young talent hoping for a break, lining up for auditions, begging to wait tables or wash dishes just to survive. Mike sang his Irish best at Club 52, a saloon in North Hollywood. He sang western and pop for radio station KNX on Sunset Boulevard. And then he landed a regular spot at the Bar of Music on Beverly Boulevard.

Night after night Mike stood before that Bar-of-Music crowd in his one tuxedo hosting the show, glad to be making $125 a week, wondering if he would spend his lifetime singing in saloons. At the Bar of Music he sang, introduced the acts, and kept up a steady banter with the audience at this continuous-entertainment nightspot. There were occasional radio appearances. Once his new agent, Don Sharpe, landed him a guest spot on a Philip Morris program featuring Ginny Simms: "Salute to our Boys Back from the War." Michael remembers singing "Strange Music" from *The Song of Norway*, accepting his $50 fee, and returning to the Bar of Music for another night's round of endless entertainment. That night changed his life.

Mike introduced a young comedienne, then returned to his dressing room at the Bar of Music.
Don Sharpe stood at the doorway grinning.
"Mike," he said, "cut the show short tonight."
"Why?" Mike asked, slouching in the canvas chair and staring at himself in the mirror framed in light bulbs.
"Because you are Kay Kyser's new male vocalist. That's why."

Kay Kyser's "Kollege of Musical Knowledge" was the number-one radio program in the nation. More people heard Kay's band in one night's broadcast than could enter the Bar of Music in a thousand years of continuous entertainment.

Apparently, Kyser had been looking for a new male vocalist for ten months. His regular vocalists had been drafted. No new singer had filled the bill. Two "hot shot agents" from MCA talent had recorded off the air Mike's solo on the Ginny Simms show and had brought the record to Kay Kyser's home in Beverly Hills.

Kyser put the record on the phonograph, Mike learned later, and played about eight bars of the *Song of Norway* classic. Then he took the needle off the record and said, "That's the man. Who is he?"

"Kyser liked me," Mike said later, "because, he said, 'I sang from my heart.' Little did he know how much heart or how many hearts I was singing from. Gen was in the radio studio audience that night and she was pregnant with the twins. There were four hearts riding on that audition, and we didn't even know it. I just sang to Gen as I have sung to Gen for thirty-eight years, and something about the song got through to Kyser. He called my agent and said he wanted me in rehearsals immediately."

Mike rushed on stage to introduce the next act at the Bar of Music.

"Keep your set going," he instructed the young singer, "until I get back. No matter how long it takes, keep going."

Mike rushed off the stage again, past his dressing room, and out the artist's entrance into his agent's waiting Pontiac.

"Where are we going?" he asked breathlessly.

"To NBC," Sharpe answered. "Kyser wants you to rehearse tonight for tomorrow's network broadcast."

"Am I really hired to sing with Kyser?" Mike asked in disbelief.

"Yup," Sharpe answered, "I signed the deal today."

Mike joined the large cast of Kyser's "Kollege of Musical Knowledge" in a huge record studio at NBC, met Kyser, sang his solos, and rushed back to the Bar of Music, where a fairly exhausted young singer was dutifully singing his sixteenth solo in a row.

"Boy, am I glad to see you," the singer croaked as he staggered off the stage.

Mike ordered another coke from a waiter in the Double Down Bar on the boat deck of the QEII. Coke in hand, he wandered to the large ship windows looking out on the ship's Atlantic wake. At the piano, a young singer was improvising an arrangement of Hoagy Carmichael's "Ole Buttermilk Sky." Mike Douglas looked across the room at the young artist and winked.

"The kid's pretty smart," Douglas said, "and has a sense of history. That was my first hit song with Kay Kyser's Band. It was number one on the charts for several weeks, and that kid playing it now wasn't even born yet."

It was 1945. Thirty-eight German divisions made their last stand for Hitler's crumbling Reich at the Battle of the Bulge. Four million Russian soldiers assembled for the final eastern assault while British, French, American, Canadian, and other Allied troops swept up from Western Europe into the heart of Germany. In Asia and the Pacific, U.S. Marines stormed Iwo Jima, and the Allies reclaimed the Philippine Island chain. The U.S. dropped atomic bombs on Hiroshima and Nagasaki.

Finally, on May 8, V-E day, the Germans officially surrendered to the Allies, and on September 2 the Japanese put down their arms. World War II ended, and music flowed across this nation as it hadn't flowed in almost six years of bloody battle.

Kay Kyser and his Kollege of Musical Knowledge was the radio band that led the postwar hit parade across America. And Mike Dowd was Kay's soloist during those next two celebrative years.

Actually, Michael Delaney Dowd, Jr. never sang for Kay Kyser. The year the world saw peace again, Michael Dowd became Mike Douglas.

"Are you really Irish, Michael?" Kay Kyser asked.

"Yes," Michael answered, standing tough and proud and Irish like his father. Michael and Gen had been invited to the Kyser's Beverly Hill's mansion in Coldwater Canyon and were discussing Mike's future on the network broadcast.

"But I can't stand Irish singers," said Kyser.

Michael felt the important job slipping through his fingers.

"High tenors are worthless. We'll lower your voice a couple of notes and change your name."

That same week, Michael Delaney Dowd, Jr. stood before the large radio mike at NBC's network studio. The band finished its opening number. Kay Kyser stepped to his mike.

"Ladies and gentlemen, tonight we are pleased to introduce our new male soloist, Mr. Michael Douglas."

"I swallowed hard and began to sing," remembered Mike. "After all, it isn't often that without warning you're renamed live, on the air, before a network audience numbering in the millions!"

From 1945 until 1947, Mike Douglas was Kay Kyser's featured male soloist on the "Kollege of Musical Knowledge" show. By Christmas, 1947, Mike had two records in the nation's top ten: Carmichael's "Ole Buttermilk Sky" and the Tobias/Simon hit, "The Old Lamplighter." "I only got $100 each in extra pay for recording those two smash hits, and at

Christmas the bad news that, hits or no hits, I was out of work again."

The NBC studio was decorated with silver Christmas trees and life-size cutout photos of Kay's singers in caroling costumes straight out of Charles Dickens. Mike arrived to rehearse the Kyser Christmas special, and entered the studio humming "Deck the Halls."

"Could I see you a minute, Mike?" Kay Kyser walked his young soloist into an office adjacent to the recording studio. Another sailor stood in the office vocalizing and looking over the same sheet music Mike was about to perform.

"This is Harry Babbitt, Mike. Harry, Mike Douglas."

Mike shook hands with the sailor and felt bad news in the air.

"Nice to meet you, Mike," Babbitt responded. "I'll run over these charts with Tom. See you 'round."

Babbitt made a hasty exit, and Mike found himself alone with Kay. Kay looked ill.

"Are you all right?" Mike asked his boss.

"No," said Kay, "I've bad news."

Mike listened as Kay Kyser explained his agreement with Harry Babbitt.

"I told him when he was drafted that he would have a job waiting when he came home. I should have told you. I just didn't know how it would end. Today, Harry came home. I'm sorry, Mike."

Kay shook Mike's hand, turned, and walked into the recording studio. Mike sat on the piano bench in the little office/ rehearsal room and watched Kyser move through the orchestra and up onto the podium.

"Thirty seconds," the director warned over the intercom.

Orchestra members lifted their instruments on cue from Kyser. Soloists and backup singers stood in place.

"ON THE AIR," blinked the red-and-white sign above the studio door, and Kyser opened that Christmas special with his folksy, "How'ya'all and a great big merry Christmas." The

studio audience applauded, Kyser gave the down beat and "Joy to the World" brimmed up over the studio and flowed into the room where Mike sat watching.

It's a long walk down Hollywood Boulevard at Christmas when your dreams have just died and you don't have a paycheck to count on. "Joy to the World" echoed out of every record shop and pizza parlor. Kay Kyser was on the air and the nation was listening, but Mike had been replaced.

"At a time like that," remembered Mike, "you have two choices. Feel sorry for yourself, lie down and die, or take a long, brisk walk, cry a while, then wipe the tears away and start all over again. There are no guarantees in my business. You may be on top of the pile one day and bottomed out the next. The trick is don't quit trying when you fall. Get up and try again."

The sign over the Bar of Music read, "Mike Douglas back for a limited engagement." In the one little dressing room that all the performers shared, Mike was getting into his old tuxedo once again. Band members were welcoming him back. The house was crowded. Two hundred people sat at tables, dozens more were standing at the bar and around the Club's front door. Two years had passed since Mike had sung at the Bar of Music. It seemed a lifetime since Don Sharpe had met him in that same dressing room with the good news that he had the featured vocalist spot on weekly network radio. During those two years Mike had sung regularly to millions of Americans. Tonight maybe two hundred people would hear him sing again.

"It wasn't easy to go back to the Bar of Music," Mike remembered, "and ask for work again. It wasn't easy to quit singing to the millions and start the one-night stands before handfuls of people in saloons, bar mitzvahs, and market openings. But if you want to eat, sometimes it's necessary to do what isn't easy."

After working the Los Angeles circuit for a while, Mike

and Gen headed east again. They visited the Purnells in Oklahoma City and Mike's parents in the Proviso district of West Chicago. In Mike's collection of memorabilia from these days on the saloon circuit there is an ad from Gussie's Kentucky Restaurant and Bar on Ashland Avenue in West-Side Chicago. The ad reads, "Tonight and every night but Monday, ISH KABIBBLE AND MICHAEL DOUGLAS, Kay Kyser's Graduates of song and comedy."

Merwyn Bogue (Ish Kabibble) had been a trumpet player for Kyser who acted as the company clown. He had found himself out of work about the same time as Mike, and they had teamed up for their "big break" at Gussie's Kentucky.

"People forget about our failures," said Mike. "They look at our success and think it's always been that way. When I was doing straight lines for Ish Kabibble at that little Chicago dive, I was about as far from success in my business as you can be. I spent almost twenty years doing one-night stands in towns across the country. Gen and I scraped the bottom just to live. People forget the long, hard years an entertainer spends perfecting his craft. They forget about the audiences too drunk to listen who interrupt your act and make you feel a fool. But we entertainers remember those moments. We know that any day it could all begin again. Success is an illusion. Fame comes and goes like the tide. You have to live just one day at a time and fill that day with all the life you can."

There were nightmare moments on the road. One Mike particularly remembers was in Chicago at the Chicago Theater downtown on the loop.

"Ish Kabibble and I were booked at the theater I had known in childhood. It was my big chance to sing in that same spotlight that had lit up Jimmy Dorsey and his band. It was a mother's dream come true."

"Three minutes, gentlemen," said the stage manager at the Chicago Theater, "and I should warn you it's a down house."

"A down house can be an audience that is really feeling glum or just a half-empty theater," remembered Mike later. "That audience was both."

The movie feature was made in France, a nonmusical, subtitled version of *Gigi*. The film was long and the audience grew restless. The Movietone News was an extended documentary on Truman's Marshall Plan to rebuild war-torn Europe. "The audience slept through both films," Mike recalls, "and then it was our turn to entertain them."

"One minute, gentlemen," the old stage manager warned.

Ish Kabibble and Mike shared a dressing room that still had Jimmy Dorsey's name painted beneath the tattered star on the door. Mrs. Dowd was in the front row with half the neighborhood, waiting for that big moment when she would see her Michael perform on that once-famous stage. The Wurlitzer organ sounded the fanfare and the little house band rose on the mechanical stage, playing bravely. But the Chicago Theater had lost its luster and the post-war audience its sense of humor.

"We walked out on that stage," Mike remembered "and Ish went into one of his comic routines. I gave the straight lines. He delivered the laugh lines, but that night nobody laughed. Ish was perspiring so badly that water was actually running down his face and dripping off his nose in puddles on the floor."

After one particularly bad clinker that had been for Ish a "bring down the house" line under normal circumstances, Ish turned to the microphone and said, "And now for the next thirty minutes my partner will entertain you with some of your favorite songs." Ish turned and walked off the stage, leaving Mike alone and unprepared.

"I whispered something to the conductor of the band and began to sing. It was awful. The band had no music, so they had to ad-lib. And Ish had left calling me his partner and hadn't even mentioned my name." Finally, the horror ended and Mike limped off the stage.

"My mother thought I was wonderful," remembered Mike later, "but I died up there from embarrassment and anger. It was the kind of experience that either makes you tough or makes you want to quit the business forever."

There were other Chicago bookings that Mike remembered with less displeasure. The Empire Room of the Palmer House Hotel was a very prestigious night spot. Mike did two shows a night, one at eight, the second at midnight. He would sing his Irish favorites for fifteen minutes as the opening act. Then he would introduce Marge and Gower Champion, who danced for another fifteen minutes. Then Mike would introduce Liberace, the headliner, who performed an hour to complete the show.

"We were booked at the Palmer House for four weeks," Mike recalled, "but we actually stayed three months. And every night I would do a medley from 'Finian's Rainbow' and 'Brigadoon' to warm up the crowd. Then I would close with 'Danny Boy,' with a celeste accompaniment. By then, the diners had finished their desserts and were quieting down. 'Danny Boy' was always a hit, and worked to pull the audience together just in time for Marge and Gower's act."

"It was a good experience for me," Mike said, "because the Empire Room was a highly respected place. And I was an example of 'local boy makes good,' you know. But imagine for eighty-four straight nights singing the exact same lines, night after night, two times each night. My manager and I would get so bored that we would occasionally go out to see a movie between shows—even half a movie to avoid just sitting in the dressing room and looking at each other."

When that $225-a-week engagement at the Palmer House ended, Mike and Gen moved back to Los Angeles for another booking with the Bar of Music. During those in-between years, Mike said, "I also emceed club dates, bar mitzvahs, weddings, wakes, stags, smokers, market openings. And in between these great dates I sang at the Bar of Music on a regular-irregular basis."

Mike finished his medley from "South Pacific," took a bow, and walked towards his dressing room at the Bar of Music on Beverly Drive in Los Angeles.

"Hey, Mike," said a patron at the bar. "Join me."

Mike recognized Carl Hoff, one of Kay Kyser's arrangers from the "Kollege of Knowledge," days and joined him at the bar.

"You still sing good, kid," Carl complimented, "real good. And you're looking good too. No bags under your eyes. Still look young. You keeping in shape?"

Mike looked at his old friend and wondered where the conversation was leading.

"Yeah, I still work out everyday," Mike answered. "And how are you and Kay and the gang?"

"We're fine, Mike. In fact, Kay has a chance to do some television."

Mike remembered that his heart rate doubled at the mention of the word. Television was everybody's dream. And he knew that Carl wouldn't have come to the Bar of Music without having some errand for Kay. It wasn't like him to sit at a bar. He was scouting Mike—at least that was the hope growing inside the young singer's rapidly beating heart.

"Trouble with television," continued Carl, "is you gotta sound good and look good, too. Know what I mean?"

Mike listened. Carl went on.

"Don't misunderstand me. Harry's not ugly, exactly, but he really does better on radio. So Kay kind of wondered if you would be interested in returning to the old Kollege for its television try."

The stage manager at the Bar of Music interrupted. "Mike, you're on!"

"Excuse me, Carl," Mike said, straightening his bow tie and heading for the stage. "I'll be right back."

Mike didn't remember what he sang that night. He just remembered standing on that Bar of Music stage and growing more numb with excitement as he sang. When the set was over, Mike stepped back to the bar.

"Sorry, Carl, you were saying?"

"Don't get your hopes up, kid," Hoff warned. "Television doesn't pay much, you know, and the old man doesn't have much of a budget to put the show together."

"How much you talking, Carl?" Mike asked, knowing he

*would take anything to get on television and out of the Bar of
Music.*

"*Well, the old man has about $100 a week for a male singer.
Think you could get by in New York on that?*"

"*New York?*" *Mike exclaimed.* "*You're moving the show to
New York? And you're asking me to pack up and move with
you for $100 a week? I have a wife and twin daughters. You
know I couldn't get a place and feed four faces on $100 a
week!*"

"*O.K.!, O.K.! Don't holler,*" *Carl whispered, looking around
the bar.* "*I'll see what I can do.*"

*Mike shook Carl's hand and slumped wearily against the
bar. To sing on television would be a great opportunity, but to
ask Gen to move back across the country again for $100 a
week was asking too much.*

Carl called the next day with Kay's answer.

"*Remember, kid,*" *Carl said,* "*it's only one show a week,
and the rest of the time is yours.*"

"*Still, Carl, no way at $100 a week.*"

"*O.K. kid, I really worked the man over. He's willing to go
$200 because of your kids, you know, but not a penny higher.*"

Mike moved to New York to begin his television career
with the promise of $200 a week. That was 1950. In 1970,
twenty years later, the same medium was paying him $50,000
a week for "The Mike Douglas Show." Mike wonders today
what might have happened if he hadn't taken that risk.

Kay's television version of the Kollege of Knowledge hit
big. The nation loved it. During the week between television
shows, Kyser and his band traveled the nation by bus and
train doing live shows for fans in their growing television audience. Then, again at Christmas, Mike got bad news.

The cast on Kyser's television Kollege of Musical Knowledge was asked to gather on their sound stage at NBC. Frank
O'Connor, representing the advertising agency that handled
Kyser's show, stood up to speak. The news he bore shocked
the room to silence.

"I'm sorry, kids, but we're closing down the Kollege."

Kyser's show was listed that week in *Variety* magazine as in the top five most-watched television programs in the country. Still, for some unknown reason, their sponsor, Ford, dropped the show and put Kyser's Kollege of Musical Knowledge out of business forever.

Mike returned on the commuter train to the little house in Long Island they had rented, sat down in the living room at the foot of their yet-undecorated Christmas tree, and told Gen they were on the road again. There followed another three years of one-night stands, week-long engagements at the Bar of Music in Los Angeles, return bookings on Oklahoma City's WKY radio and television—solo spots, commercial jingles, and whatever job could be dug up to keep food on the table and the rent paid.

Mike Douglas sat in the Double Down Bar on the QEII sipping Coke and listening to the young man playing at the piano bar nearby.

"Hear that?" said Douglas, pointing at the kid ad-libbing at the piano. "He's just finished a medley of Irish tunes aimed in my direction."

"O Danny boy, the pipes, the pipes are calling . . ."

With a touch of Irish brogue, the piano player began to sing Mike's song. Douglas watched him across the room filled with smoke-grey haze.

"That's me," Mike said, "twenty years ago. On the road. Singing for anybody who would listen. Smiling until my face hurt. Performing every chance I got, hoping someone would give me the break I needed. For sixteen years after the service Gen and I traveled the country, trying to make it big and wondering always if we would make it."

The piano player finished the Irish medley. Mike applauded. A few others in the bar clapped politely. Others nodded in the piano's direction. Most hadn't even heard the medley or noticed the young man who performed it.

"There are a million piano players like him," Mike said, "and singers and dancers and actors with amazing talent who travel the saloon circuit, hoping to be discovered. Only one or two of that million has a chance and still they travel. Still they sing and dance and act on crummy little stages in saloons and schools and market openings—even on street corners or in theater lobbies. I look back on those days and wonder, what kept us going? What got us through?" Mike paused and looked at the boy at the piano. "I don't know if I could do it all over again."

Mike got up from the table and walked towards the exit of the Double Down Room. He passed the piano bar, then stopped and turned to the pink-cheeked young man sitting there.

"Good job, kid. You sing with the soul of an Irishman."

"I am Irish, sir, from Ballybunion in County Limerick."

"Well, good luck to ya, laddie," Mike said in his best Hollywood-Irish accent. Then he placed a five-dollar bill in the coin-filled mug on the piano bar.

"Thank you, Mr. Douglas. Have a good cruise, sir."

The boy smiled. His shoulders straightened. He turned to the piano again and began to sing of County Limerick and a girl waiting there.

Mike Douglas walked the boat deck to his Trafalgar Suite. Songs of Ireland echoed in the evening air, and Mike remembered another pink-cheeked Irish kid from Chicago thirty-six years before, singing his heart out at saloons across the country, waiting for sixteen long years, wondering if he would ever really make it. If he had to, he knew he would do it all again.

There are great artists who mesmerize us when they perform on the stage or screen. They have dedicated their lives to perfecting their entertainment craft. But sometimes we forget that behind those performances are artists who also think deeply about life. That's why a talk show can be more than entertainment. When I interview a guest I try to get past the surfaces to discover the inner secrets of the successful artist's life.

MIKE DOUGLAS

. . . the stage has its own laws. Something has to be created beyond the mere repetition of movements learnt in rehearsal. My attitude has never changed. I cannot imagine feeling lackadaisical about a performance. I treat each encounter as a matter of life and death. The one important thing I have learned over the years is the difference between taking one's work seriously and taking oneself seriously. The first is imperative and the second disastrous . . . As for myself, I need to have a purpose in life, and for that I might sacrifice some of the luxuries that I enjoy; fortunately I am fairly adaptable. I try to be aware, flexible, and unbiased in my thinking. If I have learned anything, it is that life forms no logical patterns. It is haphazard and full of beauties which I try to catch as they fly by, for who knows whether any of them will ever return.

MARGOT FONTEYN

Chapter Five

GEN DOUGLAS ENTERED THE POSH QUEEN'S GRILL on the
boat deck of the QEII. A tuxedo-clad maître d' escorted her
to a table by the large picture windows overlooking the North
Atlantic. The menu included caviar and pâté de foie gras,
chilled gazpacho, poached salmon, and rack of lamb. The different courses ended with a dessert tray of elegant pastries
baked on board that day.

"It hasn't always been this way." Gen looked up from the
menu, smiling. "I don't complain about the past. You learn
a lot from those moments, but . . . we ate a lot of bologna
sandwiches and drank gallons of milk during those first twenty
years of feast or famine. Sometimes there was steak, but most
of the time we ate spaghetti, or hamburgers, or leftover stew."
She ordered French onion soup with the duckling, and leaned
back in the comfortable booth to await her meal.

"That Trafalgar Suite we are living in for the cruise," Mike
had said earlier, "costs $225,000 to rent for the eighty-day
round-the-world cruise. Of course, we're not paying the $17,500
it would cost for the week's crossing, because the Cunard Line
is using our appearances as a promotional venture. But imagine
it," he had exclaimed. "We're living in a suite that costs twice
as much to rent for one week than our first house in Los
Angeles cost to build. In fact," he had recalled, "during our

85

first five years on the saloon circuit, we couldn't afford any house at all—we lived in one rented room after another."

Gen had her own hilarious and heartbreaking memories of Mike's first fifteen years on the saloon circuit.

"He came home from the Navy with a dream of moving from Oklahoma City to Hollywood and making it big on his first try. WKY offered him his old job, but Mike was restless. He wanted to leave Oklahoma, to drive to California, to get an agent and become a star. 'Gen,' he told me, 'I can't stay here in Oklahoma City and sing at WKY again. Earl Carroll offered me a job in his supper club. Hollywood people, directors, producers, agents would hear me there.'

"There were two stories out of Mike's past," Gen continued, "that haunted him. On the porch that day he told me those two stories again. . . ."

Mike sat beside her on the swing.

"When I was a little boy, my dad got an offer from the Canadian Pacific Railroad. It meant a big promotion and a chance to advance, but he didn't take it. Mom was too worried about leaving Chicago. The family had roots there. The kids were in school. Moving to Canada was a risk and my dad and mom decided not to take that risk. My dad has spent the rest of his life regretting that decision."

Gen watched her young husband as he sat beside her on the swing. His dream was contagious. She knew that it was a risk leaving Oklahoma City and the good steady job at WKY. She wanted to live near her family, to stay in the town of her birth, but she couldn't get in the way of her husband's dream.

"Besides," said Mike, out of the swing and pacing again. "My dad told me that if I wanted to play in the big leagues, I should go where the big leaguers play. For Dad, entertainment was centered on one coast or the other—New York or Los Angeles. Nothing less would do. He was right, Gen. Oklahoma City is not the place."

Gen took his hand and pulled him back down on the swing. "So let's pack," she said. "What are we waiting for?"

"It was hard for me not to argue the reasons against that long, risky trip," remembered Gen. He had sung one song at Earl Carroll's and that quick job offer Carroll had given him was certainly not a guarantee that Mike would get the Carroll job—let alone succeed in show business. But I kept quiet.

"I think a woman should give her man the chance to follow his dreams. I had dreams of my own, but I couldn't say, 'Don't go to the coast.' A man needs to follow his dreams, and a woman needs to follow her man. I'm sorry if that sounds old-fashioned, but I believe it still. You pay a big price to follow a man's dreams, but you pay a bigger price when you help destroy his dreams forever."

"You mean you don't mind moving?" Mike turned and took her hands in his.

"Sure I mind it," Gen answered. "I'm nineteen years old. California is hundreds and hundreds of miles away, and I'm pregnant, but let's go anyway."

Mike did a classic double-take on that one. He was so excited about California that it took about two beats for the news to sink in.

"You're what?" he said.

"You heard me," Gen answered, grinning broadly. "I'm pregnant. You know, like in having a baby."

Mike took her in his arms.

It was a long, tiring train ride to California, over the Rockies and through the desert wasteland. Gen was miserably pregnant. Mike was broke. They arrived in California with a few hundred dollars to finance their chance at fame and fortune. Because of his new agent, Mike lost the Earl Carroll job, but pounded the streets day and night until he landed the host/singer spot at the Bar of Music.

One afternoon soon after their arrival in California, Mike sat in a gynecologist's office, reading the entertainment section of the *Los Angeles Times*. Gen's doctor had suspected something different about Gen's pregnancy and now, six weeks before she was due to deliver, had asked her to come in for some tests and an x-ray.

"Mike was the only man in the waiting room," Gen remembered later. "All the rest of the people there were women in various stages of pregnancy. But Mike had insisted on going along, and in that room full of expectant mothers he looked terribly out of place. Even though he hid behind a newspaper, the women kept nodding and smiling at him."

A nurse walked back into the office from the x-ray processing lab with a large negative in her hands.

"Look at this," the nurse said to a receptionist quietly. "That cute little teenager is going to have twins."

The nurse didn't see Mike, still hiding behind his paper, but Mike heard the whisper and dropped the paper fast. He had watched the women entering and departing that room for thirty minutes. There had been no "cute little teenagers" in that office—except Gen!

The receptionist held up the x-ray against the light to get a closer look.

"Sure enough," she grinned. "It's twins, all right."

Gen returned to the waiting room a few minutes later.

"We can go now. The doctor said he would phone us when or if he learns anything from the x-rays."

Mike looked a little strange, but he didn't say anything.

Gen was making sandwiches in the kitchen the next day when Dr. McCarthy phoned. Mike grabbed Gen around the waist and tried to get his ear down to hers to hear the news.

"Mrs. Dowd," they both heard, "Congratulations, you're going to have twins."

Gen just dropped the phone and squealed.

"We're going to have twins, Mike. Two of them!"

"I know how many twins are," Mike shouted back, grabbing her and lifting her off the floor as far as her enlarged condition would permit.

They laughed and cried and jumped around the room hysteri-

cally while the phone dangled off the hook and the doctor's voice continued plaintively, "Hello, Mrs. Dowd? Mr. Dowd?"

"We danced around the room while the doctor waited," Gen said. "He probably thought we had gone crazy. We were having twins, imagine it. Nineteen. Newly married. My husband didn't even have a job. We had just moved to California to take the biggest risk of our lives. Then came the news that I was pregnant with twins. Why we felt so happy that day I'll never know. But we did.

"I suppose you can credit that moment to our youthfulness. We couldn't comprehend the risk. We knew that being together made us invincible. It may sound trite to say, 'We are together and that is enough.' But it was true then—and it is still true today.

"Those wonderful notions may seem naive and romantic but they really help when reality sets in . . . and reality always sets in. Our first reality was a tiny room rented us out of the generosity of one of the Sons of the Pioneers. We lived upstairs over the small house already crowded with our landlord, his wife, his three children, and his mother-in-law. Knowing that our small family would soon double, Mike went searching for a larger apartment. We found another room, with cooking privileges, over a house on Hoover Street in downtown Los Angeles."

Gen stood over the ironing board pressing Mike's tuxedo shirt. He stood bare-chested in the doorway watching her, loving her, waiting for his shirt, and humming scales to warm up his voice for the evening show.

"People ask me where I get my clothes pressed," he told her.

"Don't tell them," Gen answered. "I'm not up to starting a laundry on the side."

"Don't worry," he grinned. "Any day now I'll get my break and we'll let somebody else iron everything."

Gen looked up at her incurably hopeful husband and smiled.

"I hope it comes before they do, honey," she said, pointing to her very distended belly.

She lowered herself into their one stuffed chair, holding up the unborn twins with one hand, gripping the arm of the chair with the other. Suddenly she groaned.

"What's the matter, Gen?" Mike asked. "You're not . . ."

Gen leaned back in the chair and groaned again.

"Yes, I think I am," she informed him.

"How do you know?" he asked, running to her side.

"I just know!" she answered with a sigh. "Call the doctor and tell him we're on our way."

Mike knelt beside her in shock for one long minute. Then he jumped up, grabbed his tuxedo shirt, and headed out the door.

"Don't forget my bag, Mike," Gen reminded her very excited husband, pointing to an overnight bag that was already packed and ready for that moment.

"My pains were getting closer together," remembered Gen. "The warning signals were obvious. When Mike finally got me into the car, he still hadn't gotten into his tuxedo shirt. So we drove full speed to the hospital. Mike steering with one hand and waving his white shirt with the other.

"Mike drove into the emergency receiving area of the Queen of the Angels Hospital, took me by the hand, and charged up the steps, pulling me behind him.

" 'Easy, Mike. There's plenty of time.' I stopped to rest a moment as the pains increased. I was in such pain that I really didn't feel like doing anything. Then I lay down on the emergency room gurney, and the next thing I knew I was in a hospital room with two nurses standing over me, each carrying one of our twins."

"They're girls, Mrs. Dowd," one nurse said excitedly. "Congratulations."

The nurses tucked one child into each of Gen's arms. She

lay in her hospital bed looking first at one little girl and then at the other. Suddenly, Mike burst into the room, wearing a surgical gown and mask and feeling much like the Lone Ranger. He stood in the doorway of that room for at least thirty seconds, staring at his young wife and their two newborn baby daughters.

"It's all right to go in, Mr. Dowd," a nurse advised him. "You have two beautiful, healthy daughters. Congratulations."

With that, the nurses were gone.

"How are you feeling, darling?" Mike asked as he walked to Gen's side.

"I'm tired," she answered, "but I feel wonderful. Look at them. This is Michele Purnell Dowd. I named her after you, Michael. And this is Christine Genevieve Dowd. I named her after my Aunt Christine."

Mike sat on the edge of the bed. First he held up one daughter, then the other.

"They are beautiful, Gen, so very beautiful."

Gen smiled up at him but said nothing.

Three hours later, Gen's proud smile faded. At first she felt nauseated. She thought the feeling would pass. But the nausea continued in waves. Suddenly her body began to tremble. A girl in a nearby bed was the first to notice that Gen was going into convulsions, her muscles contracting violently. Gen twisted and turned on the bed in agony. The roommate rang for a nurse, and the night nurse immediately summoned the hospital emergency team.

Mike still remembers the moment Gen's nurse called to report Gen's condition.

"I remember sobbing openly in the car on the way to the hospital. I was driving seventy miles an hour and crying until I could hardly see through the windshield for my tears. I knew it was serious. It was a terrible feeling. I cried and drove and prayed. 'Dear Lord, please don't let anything happen to my Genevieve. Please help her live.' "

When Mike got to the hospital, Gen was lying on her bed, her blank eyes staring. It looked like she was dead. He knelt beside the bed, took hold of her hand, and prayed again. "Lord, please, not Genevieve. She is young. I need her. The twins need her. God, please don't let my darling die."

"I was praying and sobbing and feeling for a pulse," he remembered. "She looked awful, the poor little thing, like she had just about choked to death. Suddenly a doctor and a nurse wheeled her away from me and into intensive care."

All night Mike waited in the hospital. He paced the darkly lit corridors. He tried to read the tattered magazines in the emergency-room waiting area. He walked in and out of her empty room, haunted by that sight of her.

"I felt so helpless," he remembered. "I didn't know what to do. So I prayed. It wasn't the kind of praying that begins neatly with a 'Dear Lord' and ends with, 'In Jesus name, Amen.' I fought with God for Gen's life. I begged him to spare her. I was angry with God and cried out my grief to him, but I kept praying. I knelt beside the bed and prayed and argued and wept. The doctors were doing everything that medicine could do to save her. I was doing everything I could do, hoping that God would save her even if the doctors failed."

"How are you feeling now, Mrs. Dowd?"

Gen turned her face towards the doctor and strained to focus her eyes on him.

"I feel better now, thank you," she said. "But I can't see."

"You can't see?" he asked.

"No, I can't see anything at all." Gen began to cry. "I'm blind."

The doctor tried to reassure her that it was just a reaction to the medicine and that in a few hours it would pass.

Mike was summoned to her side. A nurse stood with him. Her doctor peered into Gen's sightless eyes with a cone-shaped metal instrument.

"Look to the left, Gen," the doctor ordered. "Now look to the right. Do you see this light I'm holding?"

"No," she said, her fear growing. "I can't see anything. Mike, are you there?"

Mike moved to the edge of the bed, took her hand, and sat down beside her.

"Yes, darling, I'm here. Don't worry."

"Mike, I'm blind."

"The doctor says it's a reaction to the anticonvulsant drugs," he assured her. *"The blindness will pass. You're alive. That's all that matters now!"*

"I want to see the babies."

"You will see them," he reassured her. *"Don't worry."* He wanted to relax her, to take her fears away, but at the time he was terrified that the blindness would not pass.

Just then the nurses returned with Christine and Michele.

"Time to hold the babies, Mrs. Dowd. Here, we'll put Christine in your arms and Daddy can hold Michele."

"How can you tell which is which?" Mike asked the nurse, holding his newborn daughter awkwardly in his unpracticed arms.

The nurse pointed to the tiny plastic bracelet each baby wore.

"You'll tell them apart soon enough, Mr. Dowd. In the mean-time you can read their names on the tag, just to be safe."

Gen held Christine, and then reached out for Michele. After a little while both babies were taken back to the crib room. Mike sat down on Gen's bed.

"Hold my hand, Mike," she said. *"I'm afraid."*

"She had good reason to be afraid," Mike remembered. "They were testing all kinds of drugs on her like she was a guinea pig. They didn't have the tests that have since been developed, so they tried everything out on the patient. One of those anticonvulsant drugs had triggered a very dangerous, blinding reaction in Gen's system. All we could do was to wait and hope and keep praying."

"I wasn't much of a pray-er then," Mike continued. "I had been brought up a Catholic, and I had learned from childhood to repeat the rosary and say my Hail Marys. I also learned the Lord's Prayer. But most of the prayers I knew were memo-rized from childhood. That day I learned to pray in a whole new way. I rushed through the memorized prayers from child-hood, and then began to talk to God like I talk to everybody else. I talked to him a lot during those next three days!"

"Mike, would you pray for me?"

Gen stared with sightless eyes in Mike's direction.

"I really wasn't very eloquent in my prayer. I just gripped Gen's hands in mine and prayed that she would see again. When I said 'amen,' Gen echoed it. 'Amen,' and I looked down at her, expecting the blindness to be gone. When it wasn't, I felt a deep disappointment. Since then I've learned my prayers don't always get immediate results, if they get any obvious results at all. However, I am convinced that when I pray God hears. He decides how my prayers are answered, but I am totally convinced that he hears them."

"For three days and nights I prayed for Gen to see again. I prayed in my dressing room at the Bar of Music. I prayed while I sang on that brightly lit stage. I prayed on those long, lonely drives to the hospital. I prayed silently by her bed when she slept, and I prayed with her when she awoke again."

On the third day, Mike rushed into Gen's hospital room after his late show at the Bar of Music. As he tiptoed into the room, hoping not to disturb her, Gen looked across the semidarkness and said cheerily, "Hi, Mike."

"Darling," he rushed to her and took her in his arms. "Darling," he repeated, tears running down his face. "You can see again."

"Yes, I can see, Michael. Today I saw the babies. Tonight I watched the sunset. And right now I can see you."

Their tears intermingled as Mike laid her back on the pillow and knelt by her side, holding her head close to his with both hands, hugging her tightly.

"The doctor said it was an allergy that passed through my system. I'm fine now," Gen reassured her husband. "I'm really fine."

"Thank God," said Mike. And this time he really meant it.

Mike and Gen took advantage of the GI Home Loan program, built their first home, and moved in for Christmas. They bought a tiny Christmas tree from a lot nearby, but they had no money for expensive decorations. So they popped popcorn, strung it on old string, and draped the popcorn strings over the tree. Michele and Christine were growing bigger and noisier every day. Gen had painted their two matching cribs from the Salvation Army bargain store, and she had dipped empty wooden sewing thread spools into brightly colored paint and strung them across the cribs to keep the twins entertained.

Christmas Eve, Mike staggered into the room where Gen was feeding Michele. He was carrying a huge package wrapped in colorful Christmas paper, with a bow he had improvised from old ribbon.

"Surprise!" Mike shouted. "Jingle bells. Ho, ho, ho, and all that!"

Gen looked at the very large package and gasped.

"What have you done, Michael Delaney Dowd? We don't have money for buying gifts. . . ."

Mike only smiled and placed the gift beside their little tree. He went to Christine's crib and picked her up and began to sing to her.

"Away in a manger, no crib for his bed. The little Lord Jesus lay down his sweet head. The stars in the sky looked down where he lay. The little Lord Jesus asleep on the hay."

Christine had already been fed and quickly fell fast asleep in her father's arms.

"A great audience, that kid," Mike said. "I sing, she sleeps."

Gen put Michele back into her crib and walked to Mike. She put her arms around him and asked coquettishly, "What did you buy me, Mike? You know we don't have enough money for expensive, large gifts. We haven't even finished paying the doctor or the hospital."

"Well, if you're so curious, why don't you open it?" he answered.

"I can't. It's Christmas Eve. We open our presents on Christmas morning."

"Well, we Chicago Irish open our presents on Christmas Eve night. So, since I bought the present, I get the right to say when it's opened."

Gen knelt down beside the large gift and carefully untaped the paper.

"Oh, Mike, it's just what I wanted," she said, grinning up at him.

Standing in the middle of their room was a heavy aluminum garbage can from the A&P, with "MIKE & GEN" painted rather crudely on the side.

"I'm not much of a painter, darling, but it's all ours now."

Gen sat down beside her only gift that year, and both of them laughed until they cried. Mike had solved both their trash problem and the problem of Christmas with his crazy gift.

Thirty-seven years later, Gen Douglas sat in the Queen's Grill finishing her luncheon, watching the sun flash across the sea, enjoying the silky, undulating patterns of light that danced across the dining room walls. She politely refused any selection from the silver tray and ordered a cup of coffee to complete her lunch.

"We spent a day in London doing some Christmas shopping before we sailed," she recalled. "And the on-board shops of the QEII have a spectacular selection of Cardin, Dior, Givenchy. There are French perfumes, Scottish tartans, Japanese computers, Lladro porcelains, and Waterford Crystal. Today I could afford to buy Mike any gift on the ship or in the shops of London, but that garbage can he painted with our names on the side is still one of my happiest Christmas memories."

Gen remembered that day thirty-five years before when she and Mike and their twin daughters moved into their little house at 517 North Brighton Street.

"It was a wonderful little house," Gen recalled, with two bedrooms and a den. There was a small fireplace in the den, and on those few evenings when Mike wasn't performing or looking for a place to perform we lit the fire and toasted marshmallows in our den, like kids on a camping trip. We made "Somemores" from graham crackers and pieces of Hershey chocolate, with gooey melted marshmallows on top.

"That little house was special," Gen continued, "because we did so much of it ourselves. With a GI loan we bought the lot and built the house. Then we painted it together. I sewed drapes from sheet material. Mike built a patio in the back, and walled it in and roofed it. Because Mike worked at night, neighbors would hear us playing noisy games of ping-pong at the oddest hours in our new patio."

The house on North Brighton Street had cocoa-brown shutters on the porch windows and a boxwood hedge near the front porch. Together, they built a white picket fence around the house and planted dichondra in the front yard.

"We loved that little place," Gen remembered. "Michele and Christine were toddlers there and moved around the house on their hands and knees like playful kittens, rolling on the carpet and squealing with delight."

Gen was on her hands and knees in the front yard of their house on Brighton Street, picking out the weeds from her dichondra lawn. Michele and Christine were getting sun in a playpen Gen had placed nearby. Suddenly Mike drove into their driveway with a large-leafed green tree, wrapped in gunny-sack material, protruding from the trunk.

"What in the world is that?" Gen asked him as he strained to lift the tree from his car and drag it up the driveway.

"A fruit tree," Michael answered.

"That's no fruit tree," answered Gen. "It looks more like a giant fern."

"Get the shovel, Gen. We need to plant it quickly before it dies."

Mike dug a deep hole, poured in a bucket of special soil, dampened the earth and lowered the mysterious fruit tree into the ground.

"Well, it certainly is a tree," chided Gen. "But I can't imagine what kind of fruit it grows."

*"It's a banana tree," answered Mike, patting down the soil
around the large tangle of roots.*

"A what?" asked Gen.

*"A banana tree. You know how the girls like mashed bananas.
You know how I like bananas on my cereal and my ice cream.
So I bought us our own banana tree, and in just months we'll
have a harvest of bananas that will last all summer."*

Gen sipped her coffee in the Queen's Grill of the QEII,
and smiled.

"Mike was a terrific entertainer even then," she said. "But
his green thumb was mildewed. Everything he planted seemed
to die before it bloomed. But this fruit tree would be the exception—at least that's what Michael believed.

"For thirty-five years we have driven past that little house
with its cocoa-brown shutters and its cement block wall that
Mike built and painted. And for thirty-five years we've waited
for that banana tree to grow one single banana. It was one
of Mike's big disappointments. He loved that tree. He fertilized
it; he watered it appropriately; he covered it when winter
weather threatened to freeze its delicate root system. He even
sang to it. Still, no bananas.

"We built that house for $7,500. One chandelier in our home
in Beverly Hills costs more than that. We've lived in wonderful
historic homes in Ohio, in Philadelphia, and now in Beverly
Hills, but there is still no house like that little house on Brighton
Street. And we still hope, every time we drive by that wonderful
place, that this time, maybe, a large bunch of bananas will
be growing on Mike's banana tree."

There are unhappy memories from Brighton Street as well,
experiences that taught Mike and Gen important lessons about
living together.

*Gen was nineteen, and she had two babies with colic. All
night they had cried, and she had spent the entire night walking
the rooms of that house on Brighton Street, trying to get the
twins back to sleep again. Never before had both children been*

ill together. Mike was doing the midnight show at the Bar of Music. Gen watched the clock, trying to hold on to her gradually fraying nerves until he appeared at 1:10 A.M., as he had done every night before.

Mike finished the show and was changing out of his tux and into his street clothes, ready to hurry home, when the boys in the band invited him to a late-night spaghetti feed.

A little guy who played tenor saxophone in the band was married to an Italian woman who cooked authentic, mouth-watering Italian dinners. Every week for the past few months the band had left the supper club on Beverly Boulevard to feast on Momma Maria's cooking. Every night they had invited Mike to come along, but he had known Gen was waiting up for him and he hadn't wanted to disappoint her. That night, Mike gave in. There had been no time to eat before the show, and he was hungry. The delicacies they promised sounded too tempting to resist. Mike joined them and ate his way through a bowl of minestrone, spaghetti bolognese, veal scallopine alla Marsala, and a wonderful dessert of egg whites cooked in sugar and whipped to a frothy delight.

At 2:30 A.M., Gen still paced the floor, now with a baby in each arm. She tried to calm their crying as the clock on the wall slowly ticked the night away. The house creaked, and Gen was lonely. She worried that Mike had been hurt in an accident. As the night passed she felt more and more anxious, and more and more abandoned. At 5:15 A.M., just before sunrise, Mike pushed open the door quietly and entered, hoping not to waken his young wife or their two daughters.

Gen had not slept, nor had the children. She stood in the middle of the living room looking pale, but dry-eyed and angry. Mike ran to her and took Christine in his arms. Gen simply stared at him. No words were said; Mike realized what he had done.

"I was just going with the band for a plate of spaghetti and meatballs," he explained. "You know how you sit and talk and the time gets away. All of a sudden I looked at my watch, and it was almost five in the morning."

Still Gen didn't speak.
"I should have called."
She nodded.
"I should have come home."
She nodded again.
"I'm sorry, Gen."
Then the tears flowed, only then. They placed the babies in
their cribs and stood holding each other in the living room.
"I was so afraid," Gen whispered.
"I'm sorry, darling. It will never happen again."

The waiter refilled Gen's coffee cup. She stared out of the large picture windows of the Queen's Grill. A family walked by on the boat deck. They were bundled up against the cold North Atlantic winds. Three children romped around their parents, and one climbed up on the rail to get a better look at the sea ten decks below. The father quickly retrieved his daring child, and they stood together for a minute looking out to sea, unaware that Gen Douglas sat in the Queen's Grill slightly above them, looking down and remembering.

"All those years, from 1945 until 1953, Mike was on the road. There were periods when we lived together in a room or apartment, or in our house on Brighton Street, but almost immediately when we would get settled, Mike's job would take him on the road again. We lived in at least fifteen different houses in those fewer-than-fifteen years.

"And always we had to decide whether I would travel with Mike and take the children from city to city with us, or if I would stay in Los Angeles and await Mike's return. Whenever possible, I packed and followed. I think that had lots to do with keeping our marriage together. People's love can die so quickly when they spend much of their time apart.

"Although the extensive traveling was a horizon-expanding experience for our whole family," Gen added, "it was also terribly difficult and demanding."

Gen thanked the waiter in the Queen's Grill, then stepped out of her booth and into the first-class passenger lounge nearby. The QEII was moving across the North Atlantic at more than twenty-five knots. She watched the sea churn past far below her.

"Mike wanted to live something like a remotely normal life as badly as I did." she remembered. "The twins were reaching school age. It was time to settle down, to find work that kept us in one place for more than one short night. But it took three more years of one-night or one-week stands traveling up and down the country before we finally came to rest. Actually, it seems like we've been on the road for thirty-eight years. It's part of the price you pay to be in this business."

Gen sat in the lounge looking out across the sea and remembering.

"Mike and I decided at the beginning of our marriage to travel together. But having the children made that difficult, especially when they started school. I was driving the twins to school, to their lessons, and to their games, and Mike was working long, erratic hours. That left little time for the two of us to be together. I made a hard decision during those days. I decided to get someone to stay with the children so that I could go back on the road with Mike again."

"It was hard, because what do you do? Do you stay with your children and risk losing your husband's love, or do you stay with your husband and risk their development in the hands of able sitters? I asked myself, 'Who am I going to spend the rest of my life with?' So I got help, and stayed with Mike. One of the twins is happily married now. The other twin owns her own boutique and is working on her Ph.D. And I'm still on the road with Mike. I think it was the right decision, don't you?"

Hubert Humphrey was my friend. He was so unlike the caricatured politician. Often on my show he would tell stories about himself or his family that made his political advisors gasp. "You can't be that honest, Hubert," they would advise him, but Humphrey simply smiled, thanked them for their advice, and did it his way. Watching cancer kill that man was one of the most painful experiences of my life. When I last saw him he was thin and weak but still full of life and hope. He was a dreamer and he passed on his dreams. Now, though he is dead, his dreams live on in all of us who knew him.

MIKE DOUGLAS

There is one sure way of becoming important and influential in the Senate: just be there. It's sort of like squatter's rights—the longer you stay, the more important you become.

HUBERT HUMPHREY

Chapter Six

MIKE AND GEN DOUGLAS hurried out of the Trafalgar Suite on Signal Deck, walked down two flights of stairs, passed the children's cinema midships and took the boat deck elevator to the Double Down Room on the upper deck of the QEII. As they walked from their suite to the preproduction meeting scheduled for 9:00 A.M., they reminisced about their incredibly long record in television broadcasting.

"When Ford dropped its sponsorship of the Kay Kyser Television Kollege of Musical Knowledge," said Mike, "I thought my career in television had ended. That was in 1950. I was twenty-five. The show was among the top five shows in the nation, and yet, without two weeks' warning, the sponsor dumped us, and Kay and his band were out of business. Kay retired to North Carolina."

"We had sold our little house in California," added Gen, "and had moved to Long Island, thinking Kay's show would have a long, successful run."

"It was a successful run," Mike said, "but not a long one. It is still a mystery to me why some shows stay on the air and others are dropped. Anyway, Gen and I left New York after that short run with Kyser and headed back to Oklahoma City where I worked again on WKY-TV as soloist and emcee."

"Mike grew more and more restless in Oklahoma City," remembered Gen. "It was pleasant enough living with my folks and feeling we had a home again, but Mike's career was not getting anywhere. So we moved to Chicago and rented an apartment in River Forest, a Chicago suburb."

Mike remembered those daily commuter runs from River Forest to Michigan Boulevard. He had pounded the pavement, looking for work in broadcasting. He had buttonholed old friends in radio and television, looking for another chance to sing. In between interviews and appointments he would walk to Lake Michigan, buy a hot dog from a beachfront vendor, and walk along the lake, dreaming about his television career and wondering if he would ever really make it.

"Aren't you Mike Douglas?" the tall balding man asked as he hurried passed the park overlooking the lake.

"Ernie Simon?" answered Mike. "Where have you been all my life?"

Ernie Simon was a friend from years past when Michael Delaney Dowd, Jr. used to hang around WGN, looking for a singing job.

"I'm still at WGN," answered Simon. "Too bad about the Kyser show. What are you doing these days?"

Mike faked a typical Hollywood answer and said he was on his way to Cleveland. Little did he know how true that answer really was.

"Why Cleveland?" Ernie said. "Why not WGN-Chicago?"

Ernie Simon reached into his coat, pulled out his card and gave it to Mike.

"Call me, Mike. Tomorrow. I've an idea."

"I rode that commuter back to River Forest with my head in the clouds and my feet dancing," remembered Mike. "I knew Ernie had pull at WGN, but not that he was starting his own television show with a mix of news, entertainment, and interviews. The next thing I knew was Ernie had auditioned and hired me to be his sidekick on his new show."

Ernie Simon was talented but unorganized. His program

rambled as he found material on his desk to use. If the material disappeared under the pile of news releases, paper clippings, and clever one-liners, Ernie Simon would turn to Mike with a "You're on, kid. Give us a song." And Mike would sing until Ernie found his material and signaled to end the verse and sit down again.

WGN-Radio was in the same building as WGN-TV. Both were next door to the *Chicago Tribune* Building. Because WGN was a subsidiary of the Tribune Company, reporters and editors from the paper would wander through the television/radio studios from time to time.

"I was an avid fan of current American history even then," admitted Mike. "During those short breaks from recording "The Ernie Simon Show," it was easy to find a knowledgeable opponent for ad-lib debate on any issue of current interest. Fran Coughlin was my favorite break-time adversary. Fran was the speechwriter for Colonel McCormick, publisher and majority owner of the Tribune Company. Fran was brilliant. He sat at the right hand of power and had a photographic memory to boot. Often Fran and I would stand in the busy hallways of WGN-TV arguing about the implications of that morning's *Tribune* headlines. I had no idea that one such argument would lead to a WGN-TV show of my own and the beginning of a lifetime career in television."

"Excuse me, Mike," interrupted Paul Frumkin, the producer of "Hi, Ladies," a talk/entertainment show on WGN-TV, "but could you make a guest spot on our show tomorrow?"

Mike had done several solo spots on "Hi, Ladies," and was glad to get another television exposure. "Sure, Paul," he said.

"Three minutes, Mike." Ernie Simon's producer signaled the radio cast back into their WGN studio. Fran Coughlin and Paul Frumkin waved Mike back to work, then stood in the studio hallway chatting.

"You know, Paul," Coughlin began, "that Mike Douglas is a most unusual person."

"How's that?" asked Paul.

"Well, he's crazy about issues, important issues," Paul said, watching Mike hurry down the hallway. "During his breaks he doesn't drink. He doesn't smoke. He doesn't brag about his sexual conquests or bore you to death with talk about show business. He talks headlines. I can't get past him without being drawn into an interesting and knowledgeable debate about national or world issues."

"He's a good singer, too," said Paul.

"Yes, but Mike Douglas should be doing more than singing," Fran concluded as he hurried down the hall towards the Tribune Building and Colonel McCormick's office.

It was one of those ideas that fell into the right soil at just the right moment. It so happened that Paul Frumkin was in the process of looking for a host for the "Hi, Ladies" program. He left that conversation with Fran Coughlin, went directly to the office of "Hi, Ladies" director Jay Farraghan, and suggested Mike as the program's new host.

"All right," answered Farraghan. "I'll suggest it to Frank Schreiber, and we'll both watch Mike's guest spot tomorrow with that in mind."

Frank Schreiber was vice president and general manager of the Tribune's broadcast operations. On the following day, Mike did his guest spot on "Hi, Ladies." He sang several songs and ad-libbed with the current host and the other guests. Both Farraghan and Schreiber were impressed with the charisma, sincerity, and energy young Douglas brought to his appearance. That same day Mike was called into the front office and asked by the Tribune's vice president for broadcasting, "How would you like to host a television talk show?" And for Mike Douglas that was the beginning of a lifetime career as a talk-show host.

Mike and Gen both remember those days in WGN's little northside studio when twenty-eight-year-old Mike would step out to greet his live studio audience with a "Hi, Ladies." After they had sung out, "Hi, Mike," in response, he would open the show with a song and go on to interview, sing and generally entertain for the following sixty minutes.

"It was my first experience as a television personality," recalled Mike years later. "I had sung and been a straight man or guest on dozens of programs across the country, but 'Hi, Ladies' was mine."

Mike never forgot Paul Frumkin's kindness in suggesting him to host the "Hi, Ladies" program. Years later, when Mike began his long career with "The Mike Douglas Show" for Westinghouse, he asked Paul Frumkin to be his producer. Paul, who was a devoted family man, declined the offer because he didn't want to uproot his family with a move to California. But Mike persisted, and year after year continued to offer him a job. Finally, when Paul's children were grown, he accepted Mike's offer and moved west to work with Mike.

"Hi, Ladies" was an important break for Mike, but it didn't last long. Shortly after Mike began his stint as host, Eisenhower defeated Stevenson for the presidency. An uneasy truce to the Korean war was signed. And Senator Joseph P. McCarthy and his Senate subcommittee began their notorious search for communists in government and in the media. Nobody in broadcasting was taking any risks—and live, on-the-air interviews were risky. So WGN decided to drop live shows and return to reruns of old movies and situation comedies. "Hi, Ladies" was canceled, and Mike was out of work again.

Mike and Gen Douglas interrupted their reminiscing to greet fans on the upper balcony of the Double Down Room on the QEII. Television crewmen were still stringing wires and getting cameras into position for that day's taping. Fellow passengers rushed to get Mike's autograph. For a moment he was trapped in a friendly mob of people wanting a snapshot with Mr. Douglas or an autograph in their passport. Gen stood to the side and surveyed the organized confusion below.

The Double Down Room on the QEII is at the heart of the great ship's social life. It is a two-story room connected by a long, curving staircase. The balcony above is ringed with fancy shops selling Gucci purses, Lyle and Scott cashmere sweaters, Burberry scarves, and Sony stereo equipment. The main floor below is a large ballroom with a bandstand at one end and red plush chairs around small oak tables surrounding the dance floor. For this special voyage, the Double Down Room had been transformed into a television studio, and a passenger lounge nearby had become an elaborate control room where the director and his production crew labored over computerized video gear.

Bob Yaman, Mike's production manager, finally stepped in to rescue Mike from his fans.

"Excuse us, ladies," he said, gently elbowing Mike towards the staircase. "We have a program to rehearse. I know you understand."

The crowd opened a way for the Douglases to pass, and Mike and Gen followed Yaman down the staircase and into a private room below. The room, normally a lounge, had been made into a production office for preproduction meetings of the cast and crew. The first day's rehearsal schedule had been mimeographed, and copies lay ready for distribution to the crew, who were beginning to assemble there in the production office.

Ernie DiMassa, Mike's producer for the past twelve years, huddled in a corner of the production office with his assistant, Stuart Crowner, director of talent and program coordinator. A QEII steward was serving hot tea, coffee, and tins of cookies to the rest of the production crew as they assembled.

"Good morning, everybody." Ernie DiMassa signaled with his greeting that the first production meeting would begin. With a quick scan of the room, Stuart Crowner determined that the entire crew was there on time and that the preproduction meeting could proceed. Schedules were distributed and discussed for that first day of shooting.

MIKE DOUGLAS ENTERTAINMENT HOUR
REHEARSAL SCHEDULE
Saturday, December 5, 1981

SHOW NO. 1

(Note: Be certain to turn your clocks/watches back an hour
tonight and every night of the cruise)
8–9 A.M.   Breakfast in assigned dining rooms
9–10 A.M.   Rehearse dancers for fashion show
10:00–10:30 A.M.   Band call: Run Pia Zador's charts
10:30–11:00 A.M.   David Loeb w/Mike Douglas & Band
11:00–11:30 A.M.   Faith Brown
11:30–11:45 A.M.   Pia Zadora on camera (1 tune)
11:45–12:00 noon   Fashion show on camera
12:00–12:15 P.M.   Andy Mann, Jay Johnson, Richard Paul
12:15–1:00 P.M.   Ben Vereen (3 tunes)
1:00–2:00 P.M.   Lunch in assigned dining rooms
2:00 P.M.   Taping Show #1. Double Down Room

Safe from their fans, Mike and Gen Douglas sat in a far
corner of the room. While the large group of television professionals gathered to coordinate schedules, review scripts, and
discuss the details for the five elaborate and expensive shows
that would be taped over the next five days, the Douglases
continued their recollections of those up-and-down days in
Chicago.

"When 'Hi, Ladies' was canceled," Mike whispered, "I
thought again that my television career had ended. Television
is a tricky business. You can be top of the pile one minute
and out on the streets the next. When WGN changed their
format, there was absolutely no role for me at the station,
so I walked the pavements again, looking for work.

"Being unemployed is a nightmare," said Mike. "In show
business there is a saying: 'If you don't make it before you're

thirty-five, you'll never make it.' Now, with this generation's fascination with youth, the saying is probably, 'If you don't make it by the time you're twenty-one, forget it!' But you can't listen to the song of the cynic; you can't believe old sayings. You have to keep trying until your shoe soles are worn from walking and your knuckles are sore from knocking and your fingers are calloused from dialing those follow-up calls.

"Being unemployed is awful, especially when you have twin daughters in school and a third child on the way. But in Chicago, to be unemployed in the winter is double jeopardy. I remember getting off the elevated train downtown near the loop when the temperature was ten below zero and the wind-chill factor was fifty below or worse. I remember standing in station lobbies waiting to defrost before I could proceed with an audition. I may be a celebrity now. But I remember well those twenty years before. Sitting in dull grey lobbies waiting for my call, getting up to sing my heart out in front of a producer who couldn't care less, hearing him hint that he would call and knowing that he wouldn't.''

Mike finally got an audition at another local Chicago station. The producers at WMAQ-TV tried Mike as soloist on a variety of programs. Nothing clicked. Mike was ready to hit the streets again when a friend at the station, Jules Herbuveaux, gave Mike the singing spot on a new afternoon program called, "Club '60.' " Then the host of "Club '60' " quit early in the show's history, and Mike was given a co-host spot. Again he was singing, carrying on ready banter with celebrity co-hosts, and generally keeping the program together. When "Club '60' " was axed, Mike was given his own program again. "Adults Only" was meant to signal to the viewers that adult entertainment would be available in the afternoons.

During those years in Chicago, Mike met and befriended a young Dartmouth graduate with a more than generous share of creativity and ambition. Woody Frazer was first a floor manager, clearing cables out of the way of the rolling cameras, but he advanced through the ranks rapidly, carving out for himself a role at WMAQ as director and producer.

"Woody drank barrels of coffee," Mike remembers, "and I drank barrels of tea. Often in the little dining room of WMAQ Woody would share his dream with me.

"Woody was crazy with excitement over a new kind of show where celebrity guests would be interviewed and serious issues would be discussed live before a television audience. But nobody at WMAQ was interested. Still he dreamed, and I listened. I had found that it pays to listen to dreamers! Listening to Woody, encouraging his dream, and adding my own ideas to it would one day pay off for both of us. But it didn't happen right away. Woody got tired of directing news broadcasts and left the station. When "Adults Only" was canceled, I was back on the streets again. Little did we know how soon and how successfully we would collaborate again."

"I remember walking Michigan Avenue in those unemployment days staring at the young executives in their vested, banker suits and striped silk ties. They had jobs. I didn't. They had a paycheck and residuals and interest; I had nothing. I passed them in elevators and escalators, in restaurants and shops. Everybody looked successful but me, and I longed to work again. Those same young executives kept me sitting in outer offices while they decided my future. They kept me standing in empty studios while they conferred about my career. I sympathize with the man or woman who has no job, because I've been there before, and I know how it feels. But you can't give up! You can't give in to your feelings of failure and hopelessness. You gotta keep knocking until one day your door finally opens."

Mike and Gen know about almost giving up. After "Club '60' " folded, they stayed in Chicago until the twins graduated from junior high school, then they drove across the country again to Hollywood. Gen carried their third child, Kelly, in her arms in the front seat while the two restless adolescent girls rode in the back.

"I was 35," Mike remembered, "and I was still wondering what I was going to be when I grew up. Driving back and forth across the country in search of a job was an ongoing nightmare."

"Those trips across the country weren't easy," added Gen. "We drove from Baltimore to Oklahoma City, from Oklahoma City to Hollywood, from Hollywood to New York, from New York back to Chicago and from Chicago to Hollywood again. Mike did one-night stands in restaurants and supper clubs along the way. The kids and I lived in motels and hotels and spare rooms and guest houses. The car broke down. Snowstorms closed up the road ahead and rain mired us hip deep in mud—but we kept going. Nothing was perfect, but we were together. We had each other, and we knew that one day it would pay and Mike would find a place to really show his talent."

In Hollywood Mike got a short engagement in the Bar of Music. Then KTTV gave Mike a thirteen-week job as a singer. He ended up by singing in a nightclub named after a still-popular disc jockey, Dick Whittinghill. Gen was studying for her real estate broker's license. Mike himself considered getting out of show business and into real estate. But he could never get entertaining out of his blood.

Mike drove his worn-out Pontiac the three miles across Holly-wood to the Real Estate Board Office where he had enrolled for a course in real-estate sales. He and Gen had decided to go into the business together. Mike joked about singing songs to his future clients such as "Home on the Range" or "My Little Grass Shack in Hawaii."

A traffic light stopped his progress directly in front of a large television studio, where a uniformed guard was on duty in a glass-enclosed booth. A limousine was signaled through the studio gates. A red light blinked over a sound stage nearby. Mike pictured that studio full of musicians and singers and dancers. He pictured a live audience and himself in front of it, entertaining. And he remembered that day in the Chicago Theater when the Jimmy Dorsey band had risen on the hydraulic stage into the spotlights and the young singer with padded shoul-

*ders and brown and white suede shoes had stepped into the
light to sing.*

*Mike Douglas U-turned on Hollywood Boulevard and headed
home again. There would be no real estate license in his future.
He would keep pounding the pavement and knocking on studio
doors until one opened. He felt like an old man in a young
man's business, but he kept trying. And within the week he
got a call from his old friend Woody Frazer in Cleveland.*

*"Mike," shouted Woody over the static in the phone line,
"I want you to come to Cleveland and audition for me."*

*That week Mike flew to Cleveland and auditioned for the
program that would become "The Mike Douglas Show" and
bring him almost a quarter of a century of nonstop television
stardom.*

"Excuse me, Mike," interrupted Bill Freedland, floor director for Mike's QEII tapings. "We need you for a few minutes."

Mike excused himself and walked with Bill onto the ship's
large ballroom floor.

"Those are your marks for the Ben Vereen number, Mike."
said the director's voice over the intercom from his booth
nearby. Britisher Terry Kyne had been with the "Mike Douglas
Entertainment Hour" from its beginning.

Mike moved quickly to a taped X on the ballroom floor.

"Begin there," said the director, "and we'll cue you for a
final move to position two when your number with Ben is
finished."

Ben Vereen stepped up to where Mike was standing, and
the Joe Massimino orchestra played the opening for a rehearsal
of their song, "New York, New York."

Gen watched for a moment as her husband rehearsed, then
she continued the story.

"Our third daughter, Kelly, was born in 1958, thirteen years
after the twins. When Mike visited the maternity ward and
looked down on Kelly's face with its beautiful dimples, he
was ecstatic. In fact, Mike rushed from the hospital that April

morning and drove across the city to tell the twins that they had a baby sister. They were thrilled, too. In effect, little Kelly had three doting mothers, two of them still in junior high school.

"Our life seemed especially complex in those days," said Gen. "Mike was singing in nightclubs, making occasional television appearances, and generally pounding the pavement in search of work. I had two teenage daughters and a newborn infant to take care of. I drove the twins to school, to their lessons, and to their church activities. I was active in the P.T.A. and in the Girl Scouts. Like every other mother in the country, I tried to be there for my children, and it was no easy task. There were birthday parties to manage, homework to supervise, and errands to run.

"The complexity of life was increased by the little tragedies along the way. How the twins managed to bruise, bang, or break themselves in the same ways at about the same time was always a marvel to me. In a porch-climbing accident, Michele managed to fall and break her wrist. Five days later, Christine fell off a neighbor's wall and broke her wrist as well. One afternoon the teenagers decided to bake a cake, and they placed the mixer on the floor where they could see it more conveniently. Of course, little Kelly chose that exact moment to crawl into the kitchen. To see the mixing process up close, she leaned over the whirling mixers and caught her long hair in the blades. For weeks after that, I had to make an extra curl in Kelly's baby hairdo to cover the tiny bald spot where her hair had been pulled out by the mixer. How helpless I felt at those times when my family suffered the common accidents and tragedies of childhood."

For a moment, Gen watched her husband in rehearsal on the large ballroom floor of the QEII's Double Down Room. Mike was reading cue cards and joking with his assistant director, Becky Greenlaw.

"Mike is so alive," said Gen, almost to herself, "so positive and enthusiastic that it's contagious." She paused. "But there are times when he suffers, too. People write ugly, untrue stories in the tabloid papers, or sponsors drop a show just as it's reaching its best moment, and Mike hurts. For fifteen years I watched him trying to find his niche in this business, and for fifteen years he had to scramble for work in miserable little supper clubs or swell saloons. And during those years I could reach out and hold him, stroke his hair and speak comforting words, but I was really helpless to take the pain away. I've always wondered how people who don't believe in God survive during times of physical or emotional crises. I can't imagine what I would do without Him at times like that. Can you?"

Mike left the rehearsal and moved back into the corner of the room where Gen was sitting.

"Let's see," he began, "where were we?"

"Woody Fraser," prompted Gen, "and Cleveland."

"Right," said Mike, "Woody Frazer. What would we have done without old Woody? After our time together on WMAQ in Chicago, Woody went with Westinghouse and I walked the streets of L.A. singing for my supper wherever they would have me. At Westinghouse Woody got the ear of Ralph Hansen, a broadcast executive who dared him to try his talk-show dream on the Group W affiliate in Cleveland, KYW. Woody booked guests and auditioned talk-show hosts off and on for six long months."

He thought the dream was ended when his one backer at Westinghouse, Ralph Hansen, lost his job at Group W. Then Woody's luck changed for the better. Chet Collier, who was hired to head programing at KYW, wanted to get a strong afternoon show to build the station's audience in that important time slot. He backed Woody's bet on talk and entertainment.

"Remember, that was 1961," recalled Mike. "Today, the talk show format is old hat. You can't turn on the television set without getting two or more talk shows. So many of them are tedious now, with the same guests being asked the same questions in the same way on the same book-promoting, film-hyping circuit. But then it was new, especially in a local market, to have a ninety-minute show dedicated to exciting banter between a host and guest celebrities from far-ranging fields of interest and expertise.

"Woody booked the talent. And that wasn't easy," said Mike. "Cleveland just wasn't a center for celebrities, and everyone had to be flown in for the show, installed in a hotel, fed and watered, and pleased. It was an expensive idea, and Woody wasn't finding the right combination in any of the talk-show hosts he was auditioning."

Woody Frazer sat at his desk at KYW-TV, a pile of resumés and photos littering his desk. As usual, three television sets were on, tuned to the competition stations. The sound on all three sets was turned off, although occasionally something would spark Woody's interest and he would turn up the volume on one of the sets. On really lively days all three sets were blaring. Woody liked to know what the enemy was up to and, like any good producer, stayed informed.

Suddenly, on one of those same sets, a new quiz program came on the air, and Woody stared incredulously at the screen. The host of that new daytime quiz show looked familiar.

"It wasn't me," Mike said, smiling, "but it was someone who looks a bit like me and who is constantly being confused with me." It was Merv Griffin, then the host of a game show called "Play Your Hunch," and he reminded Woody Frazer of his friend from Chicago, Mike Douglas. "Now and then it's an advantage to have a familiar face," Mike confessed. "Not all the time, but sometimes, and this time really paid for me."

The phone rang backstage at Whittinghill's.
"It's for you Mike. Somebody calling long distance."
Mike left his dressing room and walked to the pay phone in the hallway.
"Mike, this is Woody."

"I hadn't heard from Woody Frazer in almost three years," remembered Mike, "but I knew from the first sentence that Woody's dream was on the verge of coming through."

" 'Come to Cleveland, Mike,' Woody ordered. 'I want to audition you to host a daily talk show for Group W.'

"I couldn't believe it," Mike said. "The dreamer wins again. He had cornered people for three years until finally his perseverance paid. And now, because of a chance glance at a silent television set, I was getting the audition of a lifetime."

Mike flew to Cleveland, auditioned as talk-show host for his friend Woody Frazer and the Westinghouse Broadcasting executives, and flew back immediately to sing at Whittinghill's.

"The executives looked at Mike's tape," Gen joined in, "and thought it was good, but wanted another try."

"When I flew to Cleveland the second time," added Mike, "I took Gen along. I knew that if I didn't impress them, she would."

Woody had Mike co-host four different shows with four different kinds of guests. Then he and Gen flew home to Los Angeles, packed, and drove to the Nevada Lodge at Lake Tahoe, a night club/casino in Nevada where Mike was booked to entertain.

"We were sitting at dinner in our hotel room over the Nevada Lodge when Woody finally found us," Mike recalls. "The phone rang and a very excited Woody Frazer gave us the news.

" 'We want you, Mike. They loved you. December 11, 1961, you are going to become a talk-show host for KYW in Cleveland. If it works in Cleveland—and it will work, Mike—we'll syndicate and go nationwide. Are you coming or do I have to come out there and drag you here?' "

One more time the Douglases packed their bags. One more time they got into that car and drove across the country. One more time they drove day and night, dreaming. Only this time their dream came true.

Mike and Genevieve Douglas

Mike on the set with veteran actor
and fellow Irishman Pat O'Brien

One of Mike's anniversary shows. Left to right are David Frost, Gen, Mike, and Mike's parents, Gertrude Dowd and Michael Delaney Dowd, Sr.

Mike with a favorite guest, Senator Hubert Humphrey.

Opposite page, top: The Douglases (Mike, Gen, and youngest daughter, Kelly Anne) with Pope Paul. *Opposite page, bottom:* Mike on location at the leper colony on the Hawaiian island of Molokai, talking with a resident, Ike Keao. *This page:* Mike's interview with Mother Teresa of Calcutta was one of the most memorable moments of his career.

Opposite page, top: Mike with former First Lady Betty Ford. *Opposite page, bottom:* Former President Richard Nixon introduces Mike and Bob Hope to an unidentified young man. *This page:* Mike on location in Plains, Georgia, shortly after the election of former President Jimmy Carter. *Top:* With Lillian and Billy Carter. *Bottom:* An informal moment with Carter.

Gen, Mike, and Kelly Douglas enjoying a relaxing day at their
English Tudor home in Gladwyne, Pennsylvania.

I first met Teresa of Calcutta in our studio in Philadelphia. I had read about her work with the suffering and the dying poor around the world. When she sat down before the cameras for our interview, I was amazed that one so small and fragile in appearance could have the courage to tackle the heartbreak and the horror that were her daily work.

MIKE DOUGLAS

I'm still convinced that it is He [Jesus] and not I. That's why I was not afraid; I knew that if the work was mine it would die with me. But I knew it was His work, that it will live and bring much good. . . . If the work is looked at just by our own eyes and only from our own way, naturally, we ourselves can do nothing. But in Christ we can do all things. That's why this work has become possible, because we are convinced that it is He, He who is working with us and through us in the poor and for the poor.

MOTHER TERESA OF CALCUTTA

Chapter Seven

THE DOUBLE DOWN ROOM was packed with QEII cruise passengers waiting for the countdown to begin on the first taping of the "Mike Douglas Entertainment Hour" on the high seas. The liner was already over a thousand miles into its crossing of the North Atlantic, and storm warnings had been posted. Arctic winds were whipping up whitecaps, and the sixty-two-thousand-ton liner, even with stabilizers in place, was beginning to roll slightly against the surge.

Ben Vereen, voted America's Entertainer of the Year for 1981, was Mike's primary guest for the cruise tapings. Vereen— singer, dancer, and actor—had received well-deserved acclaim for his role in Bob Fosse's film, *All That Jazz*. Gingerly he was testing the ship's roll, analyzing every possible way the deck could move during his dance number for the taping. Pia Zadora, the 1981 Golden-Globe-Award-winning singer- actress and another of Mike's guests, stood beside Vereen on the deck, wondering how the movement of the ship would affect her own complicated dance routines.

Joe Massimino, Mike's conductor for more than a dozen years, put on headsets and motioned band members into place. Becky Greenlaw renumbered the cue cards with Bill Freedland, then returned to the control room for the final countdown. Bob Yaman was snapping publicity pictures while Ernie Di- Massa and Stuart Crowner conferred with director Terry Kyne.

"Fifteen seconds to countdown." Becky's voice echoed across the room. The audience grew silent. The dancers hurried into place for their opening routine. Backstage, Mike Douglas was receiving a final makeup check from his long-time friend and makeup man, Jim Ruffino.

"How do you think the surge will affect the dancers?" Jim asked his boss.

"These guys are pros," Mike answered. "Ben's been up rehearsing since 5:30 A.M. He knows every possible way the ship could move and how to compensate for it. And Pia Zadora and the dancers don't even seem nervous about the movement."

"10, 9, 8, 7 . . ."

Becky began the final countdown.

"6, 5, 4 . . ."

Cameramen rushed cameras into final positions. Floormen scurried ahead, dragging cable out of harm's way.

"3, 2, 1 . . ."

"And now, ladies and gentlemen, our host for the 'Mike Douglas Entertainment Hour,' MIKE DOUGLAS!"

The audience applauded enthusiastically. The band fanfared Mike's entrance. Curtains parted. Mike Douglas stepped into the spotlight ready to perform, when over the intercom thundered the director's voice.

"Cut!"

The announcer's mike had misbehaved. High, squealing feedback had destroyed take one. Mike Douglas, sensing the audience's disappointment, walked to stage center.

"Well, folks, that's our show," he announced. "Thank's for stopping by."

The crowd laughed. The tension was broken. Dancers, musicians, and guest artists whose precious adrenaline flow had been interrupted by the sudden break in pace relaxed into their ready places again. Technicians tested and retested the ailing microphone. In the control room the primary and secondary tape machines were rewound and ready. Cameras went back to their original title positions. And Mike stood stage center, entertaining the crowd, while his crew prepared for take two of the "Entertainment Hour."

Gen Douglas leaned forward in her seat at the edge of the Double Down Room. From where she sat she could see the live performance on the ship's makeshift stage and watch a color video monitor of the show's taping as well. Gen Douglas had been in the audience watching her husband and his guests perform since that first day, December 11, 1961, when Mike began his long-running "Mike Douglas Show."

"Those first days in Cleveland were a long way from video taping on location in the splendid luxury of the QEII," Gen remembered. "One of Mike's first guests in those days was a trained bear named Rudolph." Gen told the story in a whisper while her husband balanced on the gently rolling stage, keeping the audience entertained and the cast in good spirits while technicians prepared for a second take. Gen smiled to herself as she watched him.

"Mike constantly amazes me. People watch him and think performing is easy. Look at him ad-libbing with the crowd and his guests, keeping everybody happy, everybody 'up' for the show. They don't know it," she continued, "but he's also watching the clock, adding up the extra costs for the delay, counting up the remaining tape time to see if the day's show can be completed on schedule, watching the barometer and wondering what the changing weather will bring for tomorrow's high-sea tapings. And with his head full of technical and financial details he still has to remember his lines, his music, his dance routines, his guest introductions. For twenty-two years he's kept his cool under pressure like this."

Gen looked calmly at her watch, then over at the director's booth.

"Oh, yes," she continued. "We were back in Cleveland during those first days of Mike's show for Westinghouse. There's no better example of Mike's cool under pressure than his show with Rudolph the trained bear. Our live audience, mainly matronly ladies, was in place. The countdown had ended. Mike stepped into the spotlight and introduced his first guest, an animal trainer named Bernard and his pet bear, Rudolph.

"Mike stood to greet them, as he stands to greet each of his guests. Bernard's chalk marks were spaced evenly down the aisle he was to walk, leading that gigantic, moth-eaten bear. The little Cleveland band performed its blaring best version of 'Teddy Bear's Picnic.' Cameras trucked alongside the bear, giving viewers a wonderful close-up of the animal's bared teeth. A traveling boom mike even picked up the low-throated growls. The lights, the heat, the noisy, nervous crowd conspired to make poor Rudolph more and more restless as he walked on his hind legs, pulled by his trainer on the long, heavy chain.

"Bernard was to perform a wrestling match with the bear," Gen remembered, "then Mike was supposed to try it. But the bear just stood in the makeshift ring staring first at Mike, then at the trainer.

" 'Well, wrestle him,' " Mike urged in a grinning stage whisper. 'He's your bear.'

"When none of the trainer's signals worked on the resisting animal, Bernard finally walked up to Rudolph and slugged the bear on the nose. Without a second's warning the bear hit the trainer such a blow that Bernard was literally catapulted up and out of the ring. He fell into the audience, unconscious. Women screamed and bolted for the exits as the bear growled and lumbered from the ring. The chain was still firmly around Rudolph's neck," Gen remembered, "but no one was holding the chain.

"Mike yelled at a technician, 'Grab the bear!'

" 'Grab him yourself,' the crewman answered, 'he's your guest!'

"I suppose that's when Mike learned most graphically that his future in television was in his own hands. Aided by a reluctant crew, Mike herded the bear into a restraining cage backstage, revived the unconscious trainer, and conducted an unforgettable interview on how not to treat a bear."

"3, 2, 1 . . ."

The countdown ended. The orchestra played Mike's theme,

and Mike, his guest star Ben Vereen, and the Mike Douglas Dancers high stepped across the deck to the music of "New York, New York."

During breaks in the taping, Gen Douglas filled in the history of those first five years in Cleveland.

"It wasn't easy to get big stars to interrupt their Los Angeles–New York commutes with layovers for 'The Mike Douglas Show' in Cleveland—at least, not at first. After Mike's show took first place in the Cleveland rating wars, Westinghouse syndicated it, first to her owned-and-operated stations across the country and then to a growing number of independent and network-affiliated stations, until Mike was pulling an audience of over twenty million Americans every day.

"But that took years of work, years of deficit financing, years of wondering and waiting and watching the ratings edge slowly upward. During those lean, hungry days Woody Frazer and Mike just kept dreaming. If the big stars wouldn't come, Woody and Mike decided they would go for talent still undiscovered. They were the first to experiment with unknown but gifted co-hosts who would share the interviewing-and-performing honors with Mike every day for a week. In that hot, cramped studio in Cleveland, before an adoring audience of Ohio ladies, Mike and his growing audience discovered the comic genius of Bill Cosby, the Smothers Brothers, Sonny and Cher, and Totie Fields. Mike and Woody invested in neophyte talent that would go on to win the hearts of the nation. Often, Mike would come up with names, now American household standards, that his staff had never even heard."

"Who's Barbra Streisand," the Cleveland station manager asked again, "and why do you want her so badly?"

Mike and Woody sat in their one-desk office above the Cleveland studio trying to get a few more budget dollars to hire an unknown, torchy, schlemiel of a girl from the Bronx to co-host Mike's show for a week.

"What can she do?" the skeptical accountant-type asked.

"She can sing, George, like nobody you ever heard before."

"And she's funny," added Mike. "Funnier than . . ."
*"She's funny looking," interrupted the station manager, "and
she's dressed like a bag lady. Surely you can do better."*

"Better than Barbra Streisand?" Gen remembered almost
twenty years later. "She did dress strangely then, at least for
the sixties, but already Barbra was way ahead of everybody
else. She was setting fashion's pace for the seventies. And she
had unique talent and style even then, but no more money
could be coaxed from Westinghouse, so Mike and Woody decided to create their own supplemental financing to get Barbra.
    "Woody and Mike began to call the night spots around
Cleveland. Imagine those same restaurant managers now who
turned down our offer for a week of Barbra Streisand! But
turn us down they did. One look at the picture of that wiry-
haired, gangly girl, with a lopsided grin and an unbobbed nose,
and they handed back the press kit and turned away. Now
that same face guarantees the success of a multimillion dollar
motion picture. That same lopsided grin draws two million
people to a concert in New York's Central Park. Just a few
years ago supper club managers in Cleveland asked Mike,
'Who's Barbra Streisand?' Now that name fills concert arenas
from Broadway to Las Vegas and can command a million
dollars a week in advance fees. In 1961 Mike finally got The
Chateau, a restaurant in Lakewood, Ohio, to pay Barbra $2500
for a week's work.
    "That was not an uneventful week," remembered Gen.
"Mike and I went to The Chateau on that first Monday-evening
supper show. We sat with Barbra's manager, Marty Ehr-
lichman. The place was practically empty, but Mike knew
that the crowd would grow night after night as the word spread.
Then Barbra stepped into the spotlight on that tiny stage.
Instead of a hushed silence Mike thought would greet this
gigantic talent, two drunks near the stage immediately began
to heckle her.
    "Marty jumped up from our table and went to Barbra's
defense. The ruckus grew louder. Barbra stood waiting. Mike

pushed back his chair and joined Marty in the fray. Before a war broke out, Chateau bouncers were on the scene escorting the drunks from their stageside table. Then that unknown girl from the Bronx with the presence of a seasoned veteran began to sing. Her voice reached out across that little supper club and broke down the resistance of management and patrons alike. Noisy conversations stopped in midsentence. Drunken jokers were hushed into silence by their friends. Chairs were turned away from tables and toward the stage. Barbra Streisand was performing her magic, and again Mike's intuition was proven trustworthy."

On stage Mike's guest star, English song stylist and mimic Faith Brown, was completing a perfect imitation of Barbra Streisand's "Hello, Dolly." The passengers applauded and the director signaled break. Again Mike entertained the audience between takes.

"Just before this cruise," he said to them, "I golfed eighteen holes with Lawrence Welk. He's seventy-eight years old and is still shooting near-par golf. I hope I can spit over my chin when I'm seventy-eight," joked Mike, and the audience agreed.

"Places!" called the floor director. "Thirty seconds til countdown."

Jay Johnson, the young American television star of "Soap," moved into position with a blue-eyed dummy for a satire on ventriloquism. Before the countdown began, Mike whispered to the dummy.

"Yike," screamed the dummy in reply.

"What's the matter?" Johnson asked.

"Do you know what Mike Douglas said he'd do to me if I didn't laugh at his jokes?"

"I bet he said he'd make you walk the plank," answered Johnson.

"No, worse," answered the wooden dummy. "He said he'd make me *be* the plank."

"Quiet please! 10, 9, 8 . . ."

The audience laughed, then grew silent. The countdown

had begun again. From her place on the edge of the crowd, Gen Douglas was still watching the monitor with a professional's eye, as she had for over four thousand hours of Mike Douglas tapings.

"I'm not a star," she disclaimed. "They give me far more credit than I deserve. I don't have the performer's gifts that Mike has. The show is Mike's—his talent, his energy, his business sense—but here and there I may add a healing touch, a word of support or of criticism that will aid Mike and his crew."

Before the nearby cameras, one of Mike's guests was ad-libbing about the eighty-to-a-hundred-foot waves that have in rare times confronted the QEII on her midwinter crossings. There were storm warnings posted for this cruise, and the guest star overcompensated for the ship's roll and staggered into Mike.

"Do you know how rough it is?" the guest shouted out to the band.

"How rough is it?" they answered in vaudevillean unison.

As the ad-libbed banter built, Gen Douglas wrote a note and sent it to the control room. Within seconds, the director had quietly discussed the routine with his guest, and jokes about the ship had been expunged from the show.

"We are the guests of the Cunard Line," Gen had reminded. "It would be a disservice to them to make jokes about seasickness or to overplay the danger of travel by ship when in fact even this winter crossing has been beautiful and calm."

Even earlier in the crossing, Gen's healing touch had been demonstrated. The television crew had gathered in their control room for another of the many pretaping briefings. One of the problems they were having on board the ship was the difficulty Mike had in getting through the people on deck. Everyone wanted to shake his hand or get his autograph or wish him well.

"We must put a note in the ship's paper," an associate producer had suggested, "that Mike would appreciate it if the passengers would be kind enough to understand the problems of Mike's schedule and not interrupt him for autographs."

The suggestion had been approved, and it had been decided that a press agent would write up the request as subtly as possible. Then, Gen had made her suggestion.

"I think we're making a mistake," she had said, smiling. Everyone had turned in Gen's direction.

"First," she had begun, "the passengers paid hard-earned money for this trip, and our lights and cameras and equipment are all over the ship. Our presence here may add excitement to the cruise, but we also add inconvenience. Second, we need that enthusiastic, supportive audience in tapings all week long. The announcement could turn them against us and leave us with empty seats. Third, Mike's success is built on the fact that he cares about his audience. He likes people. He likes to be with them. He gives them energy and they give back energy in return. Don't separate Mike from his audience. Offer them a daily time in the ship's lounge when Mike will be there for pictures or autographs. Then explain that he needs the rest of the day for production."

Immediately, the wisdom in Gen's suggestion had been agreed upon by the cast and crew. Every afternoon at three o'clock Mike had been meeting hundreds of fans on the QEII. He would chat with them, autograph their passports, and pose for amateur photographers getting Polaroid shots of Mike Douglas to share with their friends at home.

"Gen has no idea how important she has been to me these thirty-eight years," Mike recounted later. "She has been wife, partner, best friend. It hasn't been easy. I have a performer's drive. I can be gruff and short-tempered. Sometimes she suffers the anger I've stored for someone else in the business. But invariably she has shaken off the hurt and returned to support or to constructively criticize me with poise and professional skill."

"The show is Mike's," Gen reiterated. "If he quit, there would be nothing left. If I tried to be a star, I would fail. Barbara Walters once asked to interview me on her network telecast, and I refused. I've seen too many women competing with their men. I'm terribly old-fashioned, I'm afraid. I don't dream of a career for me. I see myself as Mike's ally, helping him build his career for both of us. "The Mike Douglas Show" has been a child we had together. We've nurtured it along together. If it seems weak, I try to make it strong again. When it seems unhealthy, I help Mike nurse it back to health. I don't know how much I've done to keep the baby growing— if anything—but Mike says I have helped.

"And look at the program now, twenty years old and going strong. Mike has become an institution. Everybody knows his face in the crowd. Nobody knows mine, and I'm glad. I've gotten what I wanted. I've seen something good be born and grow successful. And in the process I've been rewarded by a man who appreciates me, knows my worth, and surrounds me with love and comfort."

After seven years in Cleveland, fate stepped in to move "The Mike Douglas Show" to Philadelphia. Mike's $400-a-week salary had increased with his ratings. In Philadelphia, Mike was eventually clearing $2,000,000 a year, and Westinghouse Broadcasting Company had a runaway national success. Twenty million viewers daily tuned in to Mike's show. Sponsors were bidding for commercial time. Celebrity guests hoped for Mike's invitation. Then, in 1967 "The Mike Douglas Show" was the first independent program to be awarded the coveted Emmy for daytime television.

More than a decade later, on the QEII . . .

Mike Douglas introduced Ben Vereen. The lights dimmed. The orchestra broke into a jazz version of "Somebody Loves Me." Mike tossed Ben a straw hat and cane. Ben caught them in midair and glided onto stage center. Mike sang, "Somebody loves me. I wonder who. Baby, maybe it's you." Gen smiled at her husband looking up at her through the monitor.

"He told me once he sings every song to me. It's probably just his Irish blarney, but I've good reason to believe he loves me now as he loved me then. We've gone through the good times and the bad. We spent the first fifteen years living in rented rooms up over somebody else's house. Mike promised me that one day he would make up for the years on the road, living in motels and hotels and guest houses. In Philadelphia he really came through on that promise."

The Philadelphia realtor pushed open the huge wrought-iron gates, got back in the car and drove Mike and Gen Douglas between the high stone pillars up the carefully landscaped drive. Gen stared unbelieving out the window as they drove almost a mile up the stone-walled drive. They owned fourteen-and-a-half acres of a Philadelphia suburb. A three-story English manor house with broad wooden beams would be their new home. The acres of grass were planted with borders of yellow daffodils. As they passed through the arches of the circular drive and parked before the huge, carved, wooden doors, Gen felt weak with excitement. Each new room revealed treasures in marble and teak, brick and stained glass.

"Our twins were grown," Gen recalls. "Little Kelly was a teenager. Somehow we had kept the family together through all these moves. The house in Philadelphia signaled at least a temporary halt to days on the road. Kelly and I wandered through the woods in the springtime, picking flowers. There was a creek that flowed through the trees. After school Kelly sat by the creek, dreaming of the boy she loved and writing him poetry. I used to stand on the hillside watching her, feeling the peace that comes when you are home at last."

The noisy helicopter flew directly overhead. Gen turned from her reverie and walked across the grassy field towards the temporary landing pad in their backyard. Kelly scurried up from the creek, pad and pencil still in hand.

"Daddy's home," she squealed, passing Gen on the run, anxious to greet Mike on his return.

Mike ducked under the still-swirling blades and surrounded his daughter with a bear hug. They both waved as Mike's pilot lifted up over their Philadelphia manor house and headed back into the city again. Gen joined her family, and the three of them walked through the tranquil grounds and into their living room.

For Mike there has been very little real tranquility in his career as a talk-show host. For two decades he was on the air live for four hundred fifty minutes a week. Preparing for each of those programs, reading briefings on each guest, carefully scanning books by authors he would interview, and reviewing the biographies and credits of the actors, musicians, politicians, and celebrities required Mike's full time concentration.

The parade of co-hosts and guest stars that marched through Mike Douglas' studios in Cleveland and Philadelphia is now legendary. In the Westinghouse archives are taped interviews and performances worth hundreds of millions of dollars in current market value and priceless as a treasure trove of American entertainment history. During those short breaks between taping segments of the "Mike Douglas Entertainment Hour" on the QEII, Mike and Gen relaxed in his dressing room and reminisced about a handful of those priceless memories.

"Each of those wonderful people who shared their lives with me and with my viewers left his or her own unique imprint on my memory," Mike admitted. "Teresa of Calcutta works with the dying outcasts of that great city. Before her appearance on our telecast I read her story in detail. Malcolm Muggeridge wrote it. His book, *Something Beautiful for God* was the result of his BBC documentary on this tiny, withered nun who, with her volunteers, walks the streets in search of the dying, brings them to her shelters, and gives them the comfort in the end that they have missed throughout their miserable lives. Her interview is one I cannot forget, not because of anything she said, but because of what she was to me that day. There was a kind of peace in her that left me and twenty million viewers staggered and envious. She had settled something in her life that most of us never settle. She knew who she was and who God was and what God had called her to do and be.

"My television crew has been everywhere and seen everything. Not much can impress them anymore. But when Teresa
stood to leave and the last red light blinked out and the studio
was empty, there were tears in the eyes of the crew—and in
my eyes and in Gen's. Why? Teresa was not sad. She was
not a living martyr full of self-sacrifice and woe. We weren't
feeling sorry for her or even for those she ministers to. I think
we were crying for what we miss in life of the joy and the
peace she knows.

"Ray Charles was another co-host whose week on the air
with me left all of us moved and grateful. Frank Sinatra, another friend and guest, calls Ray Charles 'the only genius in
the music business.' Blind from an accident when he was seven
years old, Ray Charles said on the air, 'Why should I be bitter?
I believe that all of us, during our life, have something happen
to us that we don't really like. But that doesn't mean you
stop living. Once you accept whatever it is that fate deals
you, then all you have to do is adjust to it.' When Charles
was fourteen he lost his parents in another accident. But he
still remembers his mother's advice to him before she died:
'You're blind, son, not stupid. You lost your sight, not your
mind!' Ray Charles understood, and in spite of handicap has
lived a life that has rubbed off on millions of us.

"Believe it or not," Mike recalled, "one of my most effective
co-hosts and memorable guests was Martha Mitchell. During
the horror of Watergate, the wife of Nixon's Attorney General
spoke her mind with candor and courage. The nation's press
saw her as a clown. During our week of interviews, the Philadelphia *Evening Bulletin* headlined her as 'The Scarlett O'Hara
of Washington.' Critics saw her as 'emotionally ill,' 'seeking
celebrity,' an 'opportunist' and a 'liar.' But history has proven
Martha Mitchell a kind of crazed prophet who from the agony
of her privileged place at the seat of power cried out to a
nation facing moral bankruptcy. And when no one believed
her, when people laughed and jeered and walked away, she
grew sick and finally died.

"I suppose," remembered Mike, "that she impressed me

most for her ability to hang in there against all of us. She saw her husband caught in a trap, and she fought wildly to save him. Often what she said and did simply drew him and the administration deeper into the trap. But it was honest. It was truth as she saw it. And even if it was one-sided, biased, blatantly prejudiced, it took courage to go on saying it!

"Dick Shawn, one of our guests that week, summarized his feelings about Martha Mitchell in a poem he composed for her on the air:

> Mrs. Mitchell's a wonderful lady,
> She used to say things we thought shady.
> Actually people thought she was nuts.
> But now we're finding out she had guts.

"Admittedly it wasn't much of a poem, but he spoke for all of us.

"There were many moments on those first twenty years of daily production that weren't so serious as Calcutta or Watergate," Mike remembered with a grin. "I was especially clever in the animal-act department. For example, Raja the elephant was a two-ton pachyderm with a bizarre sense of humor and a horrible sense of timing.

"I can still hear his turbaned trainer intoning to the audience, 'And now, to demonstrate the gentleness of Raja, we will ask Meester Douglas to place his head under Raja's right leg. So that Meester Douglas will not worry, we will first show Raja's sensitivity with a large melon the shape of Meester Douglas's head.'

"The old melon joke was bad enough, but then they lowered a very oddly shaped watermelon to the ground. My drummer rolled a perfect fanfare, and Raja squashed the melon to blood-red juice with one clumsy movement.

"'Sorry, Meester Douglas, this time Raja will not make same mistake. Lower head, please.'

"There were times I wondered how I got into this business. Other times I wondered how I would get out alive. That was one of those times. Always the consummate performer, I put my head on the studio floor. That big beast stood above me and gently rubbed the top of my head with his melon-squashing foot. I was, to say the least, relieved.

"Robert Goulet didn't fare so well with our dancing bear," Mike recalled. "Like I approached Raja's foot, my brave co-host approached a very large Alaskan bear, at the trainer's invitation, to dance. Something about Goulet got the bear excited. He picked up my co-host, swung him around the room, then threw him to the floor and sat on his head. The crowd loved it. Goulet still remembers, with quite the opposite emotion, how he felt about me and my show that day.

"Animals are temperamental and untrustworthy sources of laughter. But the human comics I have interviewed have almost never failed. There have been a parade of them: Danny Thomas, Bill Cosby, Don Rickles, Totie Fields, Mel Brooks, Red Skelton, George Burns, Milton Berle, Groucho Marx, Mason Reese, Stiller and Meara, Buddy Hackett, and the Smothers Brothers. I can't begin to name the comics who have kept me laughing through the years. For example, Victor Borge has a gift for one-liners that never stops. He is, in fact, a virtuoso pianist, but when he hikes his overlong tuxedo tails over the piano bench and begins to ad-lib, I die laughing.

"When I asked Victor Borge who taught him to play the piano, he answered, 'My sister taught me how to play the "Minute Waltz." Unfortunately, I can only play thirty seconds of it because she was just my half sister.'

"Don't underestimate the gift of laughter." Mike advised in his dressing room on the QEII. "The people who help us laugh and cry and feel during times like these are very valuable folks. I'm tired of all the criticism leveled against actors, writers, directors, producers, dancers, choreographers—the craftsmen and technicians who make up the entire entertainment industry. These poor people have been fighting the critics since the Middle Ages and before. Greek actors were stoned in the streets. Oliver Cromwell closed down the stages of England because he said they were sinful, then he went on to become a despot and tyrant on his own—free from their criticism.

"I know I'm defensive. I know, too, that theater people have monumental egos to feed. In the process they may fall prey to drugs or booze or irresponsible sex. They may produce x-rated junk for a buck to survive. They may model lifestyles that are less than exemplary. But their craft has been important to civilization from the beginning."

"Need you in a minute, Mr. Douglas." A young floor director started the countdown. Douglas excused himself for a makeup touch-up and headed back to the QEII studios where the crowds were waiting.

Gen sat in silence for a moment. "Mike knows almost everybody in this business," she said thoughtfully, "not just as an interviewer but in varying degrees as a friend. He's talked to them all: Lucille Ball and Desi Arnaz, Fred Astaire and Gene Kelly, Eartha Kitt and Pearl Bailey, Marlon Brando, Francis Coppolla, Jack Benny, Sid Caesar and Judy Canova, Hoagy Carmichael, Henry Fonda, Elizabeth Taylor, Frank Sinatra, Gregory Peck. Maybe six thousand guests, and each of them gets under Mike's skin in a unique way. He feels their pressures and he understands why so many of them have made bad choices and as a consequence have suffered pain and grief. Today, for some reason or other, he's feeling those memories and hurting from them."

After another taped segment, Mike returned to the dressing room and told one of the thousands of stories that best illustrate his personal involvement with his guests.

"My little Kelly had a record player," Mike began, "and day and night she played one record over and over until it nearly drove me wild. Her bedroom backed up to my bath in those days, and I would hear continuously the lyrics, 'Knock three times.' It seemed to be the limit of the lyricist's skills. 'Knock three times'—and after a few days of it I knocked three times on Kelly's wall and asked her what in the world she was playing.

" 'That's Tony Orlando and Dawn,' she answered, looking at me as though I had just crawled out from under a rock.

Here I was, an Emmy-award-winning talk-show host, with an army of talent scouts, press agents, clipping services, and media monitors, and my daughter knows more about what's "really big" than all of them together. She played me Tony's version of 'Tie a Yellow Ribbon' Round the Old Oak Tree,' and began to humiliate me into booking Orlando for 'The Mike Douglas Show.'

"Tony made his first national television appearance on my show," remembered Mike. "Then suddenly he was a hit, with a CBS television series of his own. Gen and I watched Tony's career like protective parents. We loved that kid, with his affable grin and his easy, street-wise style. One afternoon at the Century Plaza Gen and I had lunch with Tony and his wife, Elaine. The pressures of celebrity, combined with a sudden influx of tragedy, were reflected in Tony's eyes that day. Soon after that his show was canceled, his much-loved retarded sister died, and his best friend, Freddie Prinze, committed suicide. By 1977 Tony had suffered a general emotional breakdown.

"Soon after—in fact that same winter—Tony was pulling himself together again and decided to make his first television appearance on 'The Mike Douglas Show.' We had talked off-camera about the tragedies in his life. Now he wanted to tell the public, hoping that in some small way he could keep similar tragedies from happening to others.

"My remote crew and I arrived at Tony and Elaine's home that day to produce a thirty-five-minute segment of a show that would feature other stars in their homes around Hollywood. After I talked off-camera to Tony and his wife, I decided to juggle the schedule, cancel the appointments that day with two other stars, and run the full program on Tony.

"No one who saw that program will forget it. Tony bared his soul. He talked about his ambition and about being trapped by television's merciless deadlines, working eighteen hours a day, seven days a week. He talked about the death of his sister, a victim of mental retardation and cerebral palsy, whom he had helped raise.

" 'My sister couldn't even say my name,' he remembered on camera, 'but she could hum with me when I sang. I tested my talent on her. I promised her that she would have the front seat in the audience of my first network television show. Then she died. Her seat was empty. And something died inside me as I looked down on that empty seat from the stage. It was bad enough to bury my sister, but then to bury my best friend, Freddie Prinze. I watched him get more and more depressed. He faked suicide with me several times. When he finally did pull the trigger, we waited thirty-seven hours in the intensive care unit at UCLA Medical Center before he died, hoping that he would survive.'

" 'As the pressure mounted in me,' confessed Tony, 'I dabbled in drugs to escape. I was living a manic-depressive life, trying to get up for the shows, trying to get down to sleep. Finally, in Las Vegas, I stood before a crowd and couldn't sing a note. I whispered, "There are two ways to go. There's Freddie's way and there is this way. I quit."

" 'I committed myself to a psychiatric institution in New York for seventy-two hours. The place was so run-down I thought of my childhood in the Hell's Kitchen ghetto. I shared a toilet with one hundred three other patients. When I tried to relieve myself, at least a dozen crazy, tormented souls would gather around shouting, "Go, go, we want to see a star go, go, go." '

"Finally free again, Tony returned to Elaine. Together they lived through Tony's treatment for his manic-depressive disorder. Together, through therapy and through love, they worked through their relationship and through Tony's anxiety and depression. Tony told it all on my show. And the crew wept as he talked—trying desperately to see through their tears so they could focus their cameras on this loving, caring, open human being.

"At the end of the show," Mike remembered, "Tony sang 'You Are So Beautiful' to his wife Elaine. Then he took her arm and walked away from us to their patio and to the privacy they now guarded with their lives."

As Mike talked, elegant stewards served high tea to the QEII passengers who had watched Mike's television taping. Crew wrapped equipment for the day. Cast members got out of costumes and makeup. The audience returned to normal life on that great luxury liner. When the hall was cleared, Mike and Gen Douglas were escorted from their dressing room back to the Trafalgar Suite. For a few moments they too would retreat—to the privacy of that little patio twelve decks above the Atlantic. Then, after dinner, the director and his staff would assemble in the living room of the Trafalgar Suite and work into the night on the next day's taping of the "Mike Douglas Entertainment Hour."

I think Ray Charles is the most amazing person I ever met. He worked with me as a co-host for an unforgettable week. Of course his music is magic, but never limit Ray Charles to his music. He is a man of great intuitive skills. I would spend hours preparing for an interview, building questions that would step by step get to the heart of a guest and his or her own pilgrimage. Then working totally out of his own gut feelings Ray Charles would ask those questions without ever knowing of the guest or his work. Ray Charles isn't blind. He just can't see. The rest of us, by anybody's standards, are the blind ones.

MIKE DOUGLAS

Times and me got leaner and leaner . . . but anything beats getting a cane and cup and picking out a street corner . . . There was never a time when I didn't believe I could do what I was trying to do . . . Anything a sighted person can do, I can do. I just have to figure out the way to do it.

RAY CHARLES

Chapter Eight

"LADIES AND GENTLEMEN, this is Captain Ridley speaking. We have just received word that the Queen Elizabeth II is sailing into two storm fronts. The first is three hundred miles north-northwest from the ship now. About 7:30 A.M. we turned south to go around the southern limits of the storm. But to complicate matters, another storm is moving down from the Great Lakes and will be in the Nantucket area later tomorrow, joining up with the present storm. There is no chance of arriving in New York tomorrow night in time to disembark you.

"I have been in touch with the Cunard line offices in New York, and the decision has been taken that we will now dock on Thursday morning instead of Wednesday morning. I will keep going south as long as I can to get around the storm fronts. Enjoy the extra day on the QEII at our expense.

"I must add," continued Captain Ridley, "there is no truth that the Mike Douglas show had anything to do with this. Somebody told me this morning they wanted to do another program. If they get the chance, well and good. But don't blame Mike Douglas for the storm. That is all. Thank you."

Mike Douglas looked across the Trafalgar Suite sitting room at Gen as they listened to Captain Ridley's announcement over the shipwide public address system. Both of them broke out laughing simultaneously. Mike had been blamed for a lot of things in his show-business career, but never before had he been suspected of causing a storm at sea.

Mike slid open the balcony door and stepped out onto the open deck. Thirteen stories below, the whitecapped seas were being whipped by near-gale winds. Spray reached up twelve decks and dampened Mike's clothing. The ship's giant stabilizers were hard at work keeping the sixty-seven-thousand-ton liner from rolling more than three degrees. The storm that would have sent lesser ships trembling on their way left the QEII swaying gently as she churned across the Atlantic toward New York.

"We've weathered storms before in this business," Mike said as he reentered their suite and lay down on the sofa. "And we will weather this one."

During the extra day on that stormy North Atlantic crossing, Mike and Gen Douglas described the toughest storm they had faced in Mike's long show-business career. Strangely, it was Mike's very success that brought on the storm that struck on January 18, 1980. For eighteen-and-a-half years he had been the showhorse for the entire Westinghouse stable. "The Mike Douglas Show" had been produced first for the local Westinghouse station in Cleveland, then syndicated to the five stations Westinghouse owned and operated, and finally to a network of more than two hundred stations nationwide. Mike had captured an intensely loyal viewing audience and had won the ratings game in markets from New York to San Diego.

"I was making millions of dollars for Westinghouse," Mike recalled as he relaxed on the sofa of the Trafalgar Suite sitting room, "but I was being paid millions for my trouble. And that was the underlying cause of what happened that eighteenth day of January in 1980. At the beginning I had been dealing directly with the able and far-sighted president of Westinghouse's broadcast division, Mr. Don McGannon. Don is a legend in broadcasting. He was the creator of syndicated programing. He fought the networks for prime-time access and won. He was a creative and daring man of integrity who dealt straight and honestly with each of us.

"Don understood the human side of broadcasting," Mike added. "When I was making $400 a week on that first try at

"The Mike Douglas Show" out of Cleveland, Don agreed that it wasn't fair that I should be receiving less than my celebrity co-hosts. Without complicated contract negotiations, he just raised my salary accordingly. Years later, when we were number one in the country and Westinghouse was tens of millions richer because of my show, Don sat down again with me as he had year after year.

" 'What's fair, Mike?' Don McGannon would ask me as we sat in the executive suite of the Westinghouse headquarters. 'You're making our company a lot richer with your show. You deserve a fair share of it.'

"That's the kind of man he was. He didn't want to deal with agents and lawyers. He refused to play games or make offers that would have to be negotiated. He just asked, 'What's fair?' and you could trust Don to pay it if it seemed fair to him as well."

During those last years at Westinghouse Mike Douglas was paid $2,000,000 a year for his talent. It was fair, but it was also expensive. And even though the broadcast division of Westinghouse was making a big profit, thanks to Mike and his able crew, they were interested in paying less to make that same profit. At the same time the Westinghouse Corporation was undergoing changes at the top. (The broadcast division for which Mike worked was only one of thirteen other corporate divisions.)

"Don McGannon was a kind of saint in our business," remembered Mike. "But Westinghouse was more interested in having a businessman than a saint at the top of that division. So Don was made chairman of the board, then *retired* chairman of the board. I believe it was a bad decision for Westinghouse, and I also feel that it led to a string of bad decisions against me.

"I don't know what those corporate giants discussed in their board room in the sky," wondered Mike bitterly. "I just know that for eighteen-and-a-half years I had given my heart and soul to their company store. Because of Don they paid me well; I've no complaints for that almost two decades of relationship. But for over a year after Don left they discussed my future, and never once did they discuss it with me present. When it was decided that I should be fired, Westinghouse didn't even have the courtesy to call me in or tell me first.

"Comic Don Rickles, a wonderful friend, called from Hawaii and asked what was happening between me and Westinghouse," Mike recounted. "I couldn't believe anything would be happening without my knowing something about it, so I answered him cheerily (and rather naïvely, I admit), 'Nothing is happening, Don. Quit worrying.' Little did I know that not only had it already been decided to fire me, but I had also already been replaced by singer John Davidson and the new show that would replace me was already being put together."

It was January 18, 1980. Mike Douglas climbed into the Westinghouse limousine and motored down Sunset Boulevard to Fairfax and the giant CBS Television City. "The Mike Douglas Show" was being produced in the finest videotaping facility available in the world. With the show's success, Westinghouse had moved the entire production to Los Angeles to have easier access to celebrity guests and to use the newest state of the art production techniques.

At that moment, in New York City, Westinghouse officials called Vinnie Andrews, Mike's business manager, and his attorney, Michael Lynne, into a conference, and notified them that Westinghouse Broadcast Division would not be renewing Mike's contract for 1981. Mike was innocently being driven into the greatest storm of his life.

As Mike arrived at Television City, other Westinghouse officials were finishing up the second meeting of the day with Mike's personal crew. The president and vice president of the broadcast division had met first that morning with Mike's executive producers, and with his producer, Ernie DiMassa.

Ernie remarked later that day, as he sat in the downstairs living room of the Trafalgar Suite, that the Westinghouse people "sat us down and told us rather unceremoniously that they weren't renewing Mike's contract. His contract, like most everybody's in broadcasting, is on a year-to-year basis. They had already signed John Davidson to replace Mike, and they told us," recalled DiMassa incredulously, "that they were tearing up our contracts to produce Mike's show, which still had six months before expiration, and issuing us new contracts, with large raises, to produce the John Davidson show.

"Following that meeting with Mike's top staffers," DiMassa continued, "the Westinghouse officials had the bad taste to assemble Mike's entire crew in Mike's personal offices on the third floor of the CBS studio facilities. They assured the entire twenty-four-person production crew that Westinghouse wanted us to go with Davidson, that our jobs were secure, and that Davidson was the 'show of the future,' the 'sure-fire hit of the 1980s.'

"All of us staggered out into the hallway," remembered DiMassa. "Some of us had been with Mike since those first days in Cleveland. We were loyal to Mike and to Gen and to their dreams. They had always treated us fairly. We couldn't believe that Westinghouse had just dumped Mike and replaced him without negotiation, without ceremony—without even a gold watch. What we didn't know that day was that Mike hadn't even been told."

Mike's limousine pulled into the artists' entrance at Television Studio as the last meeting with his crew was being dismissed by the Westinghouse officials. Frank Miller met Mike at the limo door as he had for almost a year and a half. Frank was Westinghouse's liaison with Mike. The bad news was his to deliver.

*"You're a real trooper to come in and do the shows today,"
Frank said to Mike as they walked past the security guard and into the giant, humming broadcast center.*

"What are you talking about?" answered Mike.

"Well," Frank replied, "the executives had a meeting, Mike, and decided not to renew your contract for 1981."

Mike stopped at the open door of a dance rehearsal studio. A pianist was banging on the keys. A choreographer was shouting instructions to the dancers. Mike stared at Frank for a moment, then moved on towards his office.

"They're going to hire John Davidson for your spot, Mike," continued Frank dispassionately.

"John Davidson?" thought Mike, as he walked up the two flights of stairs to his office, "He just doesn't seem the type."

"John and I had been friends for years," Mike recalled. "Or at least acquaintances, through his appearances on my show. I liked the clean-faced kid with his bright eyes and crooner voice. But he didn't seem right for a talk show. I remember now how businesslike I was even as the shock settled into me. Trying to work out the pros and cons of my replacement while still not believing I had been replaced.

"I remember too," continued Mike, "as I walked those television production corridors that morning, how crew members looked at me with grief and surprise in their eyes. I felt like a man at his own funeral, but until Frank blurted out the news, I hadn't even known why everyone around seemed so glum.

"I am a student of broadcast history," Mike says. "You have to understand broadcasting to succeed in this business. I had heard about the shabby way others like me had been treated by management in days past. Red Skelton, the pioneer in live television who built a network with his blood, sweat and laughter, was just dumped—never even notified officially. The same kind of thing happened to Garry Moore, the granddaddy of the game show hosts, and to Arthur Godfrey, the mainstay of variety broadcasting. When the corporate offices were through with the people whose talent had supported their teak-paneled boardrooms and their gold-and-marble reception halls, those people were simply discarded like old Kleenex.

"I just never dreamed that after eighteen-and-a-half years it would happen to me. I wandered into my office in a daze. Ernie DiMassa was standing there. Ernie is six foot, six inches tall, but he slumped up against the wall in shock.

" 'How could they do it to you,' he asked, 'after so long?'

"We stood silently for a moment, lost in the same question. Other crew members gathered in the doorway. No one spoke as the word rippled out that only at that moment had I learned of my replacement. Finally I said to that loyal bunch of skilled and loving people, 'Well, we have two ninety-minute shows to do today. Let's get at it. Then we'll talk.' "

"I began that morning like every other morning of the year," remembered Gen. "Mike and I had breakfast, read the papers, discussed the children, and talked shop about taping upcoming guests and remote location schedules. Mike was hardly out the door when the telephone rang. It was Paul Frumkin, one of Mike's friends and long-time associates—the one who had recommended Mike to host 'Hi, Ladies' back in Chicago."

Paul Frumkin's voice was shaky. "Gen," he said, "is Mike still there?"

"No," Gen answered him. "He's been picked up by the limousine. Is something the matter?"

"Westinghouse has decided not to renew Mike's option for 1981," Paul announced glumly, "They're going to do a show with John Davidson instead."

"I can't believe it," Gen whispered into the phone.

"We just heard," Frumkin continued. "I've checked out the news with every trustworthy source I could find. It looks true, Gen. Mike's been dumped."

"Does Mike know?" Gen asked him. "Has Mike been told?"

"Not unless they reached him on the Westinghouse limo phone. And that's unlikely," he replied.

"Call him immediately," she urged Frumkin. "As soon as he gets to the studio. Be sure that he's all right. I'll call Vinnie in New York."

"When I reached our business manager, Vinnie Andrews, in New York," said Gen, "I told him what had happened in California. He was shocked. Mike was supposed to be the first to know. Westinghouse had promised to make the announcement later, but something had obviously gone wrong.

"I instructed Vinnie to get our press people working on a news release to station owners, managers, and time buyers stating clearly that Mike was not quitting show business, no matter what they heard to the contrary. Then I called our agency people, Rogers and Cowan, telling them to get in touch with Mike about designing a campaign to explain Mike's side of the dismissal story.

"Westinghouse dared to release a press announcement that day that 'Mike Douglas [was] retiring from his Emmy-award-winning series' and that 'John Davidson [was] stepping in to replace Mike.' But we got two hundred telegrams out to those same station managers that same day telling them Westinghouse's announcement was untrue and fabricated! Not only would Mike be continuing 'The Mike Douglas Show,' we said, but he would be making it available to their stations.

"The Westinghouse announcement was humiliating," remembered Mike. "Westinghouse orchestrated a press campaign using the word 'dump.' Mike Douglas has been 'dumped,' they said. It really hurt me. I confess it. I staggered around the studio that day, performing every line on cue but reeling from the dirty treatment I had been given. I was muttering to myself about their cold, calculating, underhanded treatment when Gen finally got through to me on the phone.

"She let me pour out my anger and disappointment. For a time she agreed. I felt her sympathy and her understanding that day. Then she interrupted my tirade with, 'Well, honey, we've done it before. We can do it again.'

"I got the message," remembered Mike. "Gen knew I would have a plan and that the plan was already in motion. Gently she channeled my angry conversation from a destructive to a constructive focus. Blame is no blamed good. Hatred simply consumes the person doing the hating. But anger, anger can be a friend. The Bible says, 'Be angry, but sin not.' It doesn't say, 'Don't be angry when there is just cause.' "

"In the exercise room in our house in Beverly Hills," Gen

added, "Mike has two punching bags. One is long and heavy, made from canvas and very hard. The other is small, like a basketball suspended from a frame. Mike punches those bags almost every day. Whump, whump, whump—I can hear him hitting the large, heavy bag. Bangity, bangity, bangity—it's the little bag he's knocking around. But both bags are there for Mike to release his anger creatively.

"Mike's dad trained amateur fighters. Mike grew up on the rough side of Chicago. He doesn't let his anger boil over into violence; he uses his anger as a creative force. But when the extra anger needs siphoning away, he punches those bags, showers, and returns refreshed."

"Anger got me through those next stormy weeks," Mike said. "I refused to let my television career be ruined by businessmen in conference in their boardrooms in the sky. But those Westinghouse executives were clever. Their technique and timing were carefully calculated to do me in."

"To understand what Mike and Gen were going through during those stormy days," explained Ernie DiMassa later, "is to understand the realities of television. The first reality is that Mike's dream had become a multimillion-dollar business. The art of television isn't like the art of painting. With painting, you need something like ten dollars' worth of canvas, paint, and brushes to realize your dream. 'The Mike Douglas Show' required millions of dollars just to pay the production bills! Mike had to come up with production financing immediately, or he would lose the creative, dedicated team he had built over the past eighteen years.

"And I say 'immediately,'" continued DiMassa, "because the second television reality is that to guarantee success requires having about a hundred stations signed to use the program, and Mike was dropped less than two weeks before the National Association of Program-Buying Television Executives meeting, where local stations gather to see programs available for the next year and sign up the programs they believe their viewers will watch. So Mike, to get stations and guarantee funding, had to create a new program and market it in only two weeks,

while at the same time meeting his ninety-minute daily program
contract with Westinghouse."

*The airport bus pulled up before the entertainment entrance
of the Las Vegas Hilton. The "Mike Douglas Show" crew and
cast members unloaded their equipment, costumes, and musical
instruments into the large mainstage area of that huge entertainment center. It was less than twenty-four hours after Mike had
been dropped by Westinghouse. They had scheduled this week
of on-location programs months before. The schedule could not
be changed. Everyone on that airplane ride from Los Angeles
was wondering the same thing. Could Mike and Gen and their
business manager put together a new program and fund it in
time?*

*They were a loyal team who had been with Mike a long
time. Many of their families had moved with him—some from
Cleveland to Philadelphia, then from Philadelphia to Los Angeles. They had invested large chunks of their lives in Mike. He
was their employer; they depended on him for their weekly pay-
checks.*

*The cast and crew of "The Mike Douglas Show" liked Mike
and trusted him. They hoped, for reasons both selfish and idealis-
tic, that his dream wouldn't die. And they were angry about
the way Westinghouse had treated him and hoped there was
some way they could avoid being a part of that treatment. But
they also needed jobs! Westinghouse officials had promised them
contracts to produce the "John Davidson Show." They had nothing against John, but they were Mike's team and wanted to
go on working with him.*

*On the temporary-production-office door in the Hilton Ball-
room, Westinghouse officials had placed a call for a complete
crew/cast meeting that same day. Mike's team of professionals
set their television gear in place, looked over plans for the evening's taping, and reported to the meeting room as ordered.
Mike and Gen were still en route from Los Angeles.*

*Cast and crew assembled around the coffee pot and nibbled
on cookies and fruit they found waiting in the conference room.*

Conversations were whispered. Everyone was confused and angry. At that moment, the same man who had greeted Mike's limousine twenty-four hours earlier and told him of Westinghouse's cancellation entered the room.

"Hi, gang. Glad you made it."

He was too enthusiastic. The atmosphere in the room grew more hostile. This was a Westinghouse man in Mike Douglas territory. They had always seen him as part of their team. Now they wondered.

"I know what you're thinking," he began, sitting casually on a desk and swinging his legs back and forth as he addressed them. "But time goes on. You've been successful with Mike. Now you'll be even more successful with John."

Mike's people looked away. The whole scene was embarrassing. Everybody felt helpless. What could they say? There were no guarantees that Mike could pull together a new program, a new network of stations, and a new financial package in time; they weren't even sure if Mike was attempting that impossible task. And Westinghouse was a billion-dollar corporation. If they went with John Davidson, they would have jobs and security. They wouldn't have to start that awful search for work in a city full of unemployed television talent. They wouldn't have to get into those long, humiliating unemployment-compensation lines. Where was Mike? Could he pull off the miracle in time?

The Westinghouse executive continued addressing them.

"Mike is a pioneer. He set the pace for daytime talk shows. He made and broke all the records. But John is the man of the future. He is young, a fresh talent. Women viewers will love him. He'll guarantee our ratings and give us success. Now to show him you're all on his team, I've arranged to call him and talk to him while we're together."

The Douglas crew stood in dumb amazement as the Westinghouse executive picked up a phone, dialed Davidson's residence, and talked to the young singer enthusiastically.

"We're all here, John. The team has agreed to produce your new show. Congratulations. This is the best team in broadcasting, and we're looking forward to what we can accomplish together."

The meeting ended. The Douglas team left the room with that awful feeling that comes from being tricked and manipulated but helpless and unsure what to do about it.

At that moment, Mike and Gen arrived by limousine from the Las Vegas airport. Quickly they called a dinner conference with Mike's producer. Then, person by person, they set up meetings with each member of the Mike Douglas team. Meanwhile, unaware of the day's events, loyal Mike Douglas fans had been waiting for hours in long lines that stretched the length of the hotel building. All the hectic business of an on-location television production had to be carried on simultaneously with hurried conferences and difficult, long-term decision making.

In their Hilton suite, Mike and Gen carefully unfolded their dream for the new "Mike Douglas Show."

"Westinghouse offered me $500,000 cash just to stay off the air," remembered Mike. "It was severance pay, I suppose— and a lot of severance pay at that. I could have lived quite comfortably for the rest of my life on what we had already earned on "The Mike Douglas Show." Add to that their offer of another half million dollars, and folding up and quitting the business looked quite tempting—for about thirty seconds. But I have too many dreams to quit now.

"Ladies and gentlemen, Mike Douglas!"
The Hilton Showroom audience burst into applause. The band played Mike's theme. Mike entered the room and began another show on the road. He interviewed guest stars, introduced musical features, and entertained the crowd with ad-libbed banter during taping breaks. Gen sat at a table and watched her husband perform, knowing the storm he was living through, praying he would have the energy and the grace to weather it.

"It was the worst moment in my life," remembered Gen, "to see my husband hurt so cruelly by people he thought were his friends. I felt so helpless having to watch him suffer. It had nothing to do with money or risk or career. I can go back to an apartment over somebody's garage and be perfectly happy. I wasn't worried about the money or the future. I was worried about the man, and about how hard it was for him to suffer the indignities of being dumped after almost twenty years of loyal service.

"It's happening to thousands, maybe millions of families across the country, right now," she admitted. "What happened to us was not unique. Men who have invested their lives in a business or a school or a company are being fired or retired because of the recession we're in. They have to return home and tell their wives and families, just as Mike did. They have to feel loss and failure and anger the same as Mike. That's when they need their women most.

"We can't give them a new job or take away the suffering, but we can be there and give them our strength to get them through that suffering. I don't think it's what we say, but what we do that counts. Just being by his side is important. That first night I put on quiet music, served one of Mike's favorite meals, and simply listened. I am confident that Mike can get through any storm that blows up. I showed him that confidence. Why worry? He was worrying enough for both of us. I just said in as many ways I could think of, 'I love you, darling. And I know that you can make it.'"

The Hilton Showroom was empty. Gen sat at the table, waiting for her husband to get out of makeup and join her for a late dinner with key production people from "The Mike Douglas Show." In less than twenty-four hours Mike and Gen were already building their new team. At the very same time, the president and the vice president of Westinghouse Broadcasting were meeting with other members of the Mike Douglas team, hoping to woo them into the John Davidson camp.

"They offered to tear up my current contract for the Douglas Show," remembered one of Mike's people much later, "and write me a new contract to do the Davidson show for a lot more money. They even promised to make the contract retroactive so that I would, in effect, be getting a raise for the past six months as well as the next six! They really worked to convince me that John Davidson was chosen because of his ascending star, but I knew the whole plan to dump Mike had been a financial decision hoping that John, for much less money, could accomplish in ratings and commercial sales what Mike had accomplished. What they forgot was Mike's own peculiar genius and his loyal audience of twenty million. Mike had spent a lifetime developing both. Mike's audience knew he cared. There was no way he could so easily be replaced."

"One by one, over the next few days, we met with the team," remembered Mike. "And one by one they agreed to take the risk and stay on board with us. It was really gratifying for Gen and me to see their love and loyalty. Westinghouse offered them financial security. I offered them, in Churchill's words, 'blood, sweat and tears.' But of the twenty-four key staff members I asked to stay, twenty-three agreed to my offer."

Westinghouse made two serious mistakes in calculating the response to their announcement of Mike's "retirement." Mike had a valid contract to complete six more months of daily ninety-minute shows. They apparently assumed he would break that contract in anger and walk away, and that his staff and crew would buy their offer of new contracts and higher salaries. But Mike refused to quit, and Mike's team refused to abandon him. So Westinghouse moved ahead and made their second mistake.

"I entered our production office at CBS when we returned from the remote location in Las Vegas," remembered one Douglas staffer, "and was shocked to discover that the locks on my files had been changed and that a Westinghouse executive had the key. I had to go on producing Mike's show with only limited access to my own files. Because Westinghouse had bankrolled our production budget, they legally owned the contents of the entire Mike Douglas files, but we were still producing that show for them. By cutting us off from our sources they were only damaging their own program!"

"Imagine it," another staffer added. "Eighteen years of materials locked up. All our research, all our talent information, all our music charts—our entire files—locked up. Every time we wanted any piece of information we had to get the keeper of the key from Westinghouse to open our files and supervise our use of them. It was like starting from scratch, and for six months we worked under those conditions."

Mike's producer hurried into their offices in CBS waving the art designer's sketches for the new sets they needed for the Douglas show that day.

"Where are our sets, John?" he asked nervously. "We're on the air in hours and nothing is ready."

The set builder held up his hands in frustration.

"Westinghouse canceled our set budget," he explained. "And they didn't even bother to tell me. Now it's too late. We'll have to go with the old faithful backdrop and hope our lighting boys can pull it off."

"It was unbelievable the lengths to which Westinghouse went to close us down," remembered Mike, "And all the time they were only doing damage to their own show. We were working for them. Our show was bringing them ratings, raves, and profit, but they were so anxious to have us out of there that they harassed us in ways petty and grand. For example, they cut off "The Mike Douglas Show" promotion budget. That was a big mistake. They needed viewers to keep revenues up. They even sent out booking agents to book talent for the Davidson Show that I had already booked for our program, apparently in an effort to make the transition as difficult as possible."

"Mike fought back," added Gen. "He was invited to make guest appearances on other shows on other networks. On Tom Snyder's NBC late-night show, Mike told the whole story to the nation's insomniacs, promising that there would not be one day between his last show for Westinghouse and his first "Mike Douglas Entertainment Hour" program. Mike made himself available to the press for interviews. Our team continued a barrage of telegrams and press releases to stations across the country. We designed the new show and, at the suggestion of our business manager and lawyer, a new format; then we arranged with a company in New York to barter it to stations across the nation. We put together a complete production team. We also produced materials that introduced the new "Mike Douglas Show," and we went to the National Association of Program-Buying Television Executives in New York to present our new show to local stations from across the country. And we did it all in two weeks' time, while producing that daily show for Westinghouse!"

"One night, John Davidson himself called me to explain his side of the story," said Mike. "He said he wanted to behave like a gentleman and so had called. I've thought a lot about his call since then. I like John. I wish him well in this business. But if the tables had been reversed, if it had been the other way around, if John had a long-running show and his backers were in secret negotiations to dump him for me, I would have gotten on the phone and called him and blown the whole thing. I would have said, 'John, they're negotiating with me to take over your spot, and I want you to know about it.'

Westinghouse had been in secret negotiations for eight months to a full year. When the pot finally boiled over, we only had two weeks to recover. But we did it."

At the NAPTE convention, where the fate of the new "Mike Douglas Show" would be settled, thousands of television executives from across the nation and around the world wandered in and out of hotel suites and display areas wearing their buyer's badges and selecting their station's programing for the coming year. John Davidson was there in the Westinghouse display area, shaking hands with station managers, and emoting enthusiastically about the new John Davidson Show. In another booth not far away, Mike Douglas was greeting old friends from the industry, explaining his new show, and guaranteeing that "The Mike Douglas Show" would be on the air the day Westinghouse's "Mike Douglas Show" closed down forever. Mike needed one hundred two stations to sign on the line for his dream to be launched. At the close of the convention, one hundred twenty stations had signed. Mike had weathered the stormiest crisis of his career.

Now in his suite on the QEII, Mike put down the day's shooting script for the fifth taping of "The Mike Douglas Entertainment Hour" on the high seas. The ship rolled against the North Atlantic storm. Mike watched the grey horizon rising and falling as the great ship plowed through the waves. He had no idea what storms lay ahead in his ongoing love affair with television, or how he would weather those storms. But for the moment he and Gen were on the road. There were lines to be memorized, guests to interview, musical numbers to perform. His adrenaline level was high. The energy and excitement of that moment was enough.

He would face tomorrow's storms tomorrow. Today's storm needed all the focus he could muster. Mike Douglas, under pressure, was at peace.

Norman Vincent Peale's books had made a great impression on me even before I interviewed the man. Then, when I did interview him, I discovered that I, too, am a positive thinker. In fact, I can't stand negative thinking. I will not have negative thinkers around me. I've hired people who say, "Oh, we couldn't get him for the show" or "There's no way to get our whole team to that remote location to interview that person." Why not? All people can tell us is no. Go for it. Don't waste time thinking through the reasons a plan won't work; make it work! . . . Giving up too quickly is fatal. Giving in to negative thinking will destroy you. Norman Vincent Peale has spent a lifetime passing on the power he found in positive thinking and I, for one, am grateful.

MIKE DOUGLAS

Every great personality I have ever known, and I have known many, who has demonstrated the capacity for prodigious work has been a person in tune with the Infinite. . . . The longer I live, the more I am convinced that neither age nor circumstance needs to deprive us of energy and vitality. We are at last. . . . beginning to comprehend a basic truth hitherto neglected, that our physical condition is determined very largely by our emotional condition, and our emotional life is profoundly regulated by our thought life. All through its pages, the Bible talks about vitality and force and life. . . . Jesus stated the key expression, ". . . I am come that they might have life, and that they might have it more abundantly" (John 10:10). This does not rule out pain or suffering or difficulty, but the clear implication is that if a person practices the creative and re-creative principles of Christianity he can live with power and energy.

NORMAN VINCENT PEALE

Chapter Nine

A LOUD SIREN ANNOUNCED LIFEBOAT DRILL on board the Queen Elizabeth II. Passengers reached into closets for bright orange life jackets, then hurried to find their lifeboat stations on a deck nearby. Stewards and ship's officers guided passengers and crew to their proper places.

"The lifeboat drill is kind of eery," said Gen. "With that storm out there, I can't help but keep thinking of the Titanic in all her splendor, that mistress of the seas that disappeared beneath the icy water as passengers in lifeboats watched with disbelief. I wondered about passengers on the Mauritania or the Andrea Dorea who discovered unexpectedly that the ship's siren was not sounding a drill at all. What seemed unreal soon turned into ghastly reality. One moment passengers were alive, dancing, dining, discussing life. The next moment those same passengers were dying, struggling against the sea that would inevitably claim them."

Mike stood at his lifeboat station reading the list of precautions that the Cunard lines had taken to save her passengers in case of a tragedy at sea. "At the center of the QEII is an emergency room equipped to keep watch on every part of this ship," he read. "At the center of the room is a desk carrying an illuminated master plan of the ship. At the turn of a handle any required area can be presented, displaying all the safety precautions available. The structure of the ship is incombustible. Each room has automatic sprinkler and alarm systems. The ship is divided into fifteen watertight compartments. Lifeboats can carry nearly four thousand people, and the thirty-two hundred life jackets incorporate a specially designed collar that ensures adequate support to head and neck and keeps the wearer's mouth at least six inches above water whether the wearer is unconscious or not."

Mike twisted his head in the bulky jacket and wondered with a grin, "What happens to my head six inches above the waterline if a shark takes a liking to the rest of me?"

Other passengers smiled or giggled nervously, looking down into the huge waves ten decks below them.

"I don't know if I would get into a smaller boat even if the larger one was sinking," said a Douglas fan. "Would you?"

Mike quoted a line from Will Rogers: "Regardless of the miracles of medicine and prayer, the ratio of those living to those who will die is still one for one."

Later, in their suite, the Douglases talked about those awful times when Will Roger's truth had really hit home to them.

"We were doing a remote telecast from on board a Navy aircraft carrier outside of San Diego," Mike remembered. "Dick Creque, my technical director from the beginning years of "The Mike Douglas Show," was as usual scurrying about getting cameras and power lines, lights and sound equipment into position for the taping. There was one ladder that extended more than ten decks into the ship, straight down. Dick, always conscious of time in our business, gave up on the slow-moving and often crowded elevators, and was racing up and down that very scary shortcut. We aren't sure if he fainted or just lost hold of the next rung of the ladder. Whatever the cause, Dick fell at least four flights and died."

"I was hosting several crew wives on location that day," remembered Gen. "One of our personnel rushed up to me on the deck where we were watching the taping and whispered to me that Dick had fallen. His wife and I rushed to the scene, but too late. She found her husband already covered

Gen took his hand and smiled. There wasn't much she could say.

"Don't worry, Sis. I'm not through yet," he said.

The attendants were about to wheel him into surgery. "I'll wait for you here," she said.

He grinned up at her again, that mischievous Purnell grin, then he disappeared into the blue surgery unit.

"Marge and I sat in the waiting room for an eternity," said Gen. "I can't think of a much worse place to sit. Every doctor who strolls through the room makes your heart beat faster and your stomach churn. Thoughts race through your mind. Questions fly by unanswered. Regrets appear and linger. 'If only we could have spent more time together.' 'Maybe if we had lived closer I could have helped my brother solve those complex family problems he faced.' 'If only he had told me, but he never complained. I wasn't even aware of the problems he and Marge were facing.'

Finally, Bill's surgeon approached us and took Marge by the hand."

" 'How is he, doctor?' she asked in that age-old ritual of hope.

"For a moment he hemmed and hawed, then got up his courage to tell her that Bill was being eaten alive by a malignancy that had metastasized and spread throughout his entire body. Then the doctor was gone, and I stood holding Marge's hand, knowing that Bill had a very short time to live and that this second tragedy would probably mean Marge's death as well.

"Marge did die not long after Bill—in her sleep. The entire family was buried in a large family plot we purchased for them in an Oklahoma City cemetery."

"My father had gotten sick earlier that same year," Gen continued, "and Mike and I visited him in the old family home. Mother and Dad never took medicine. They would use an occasional aspirin, and Dad loved mother to rub his shoulders with Sloan's linament, but medicines and vitamin pills were all wasted on those two."

William Purnell, Sr. lay in his bed, hardly a line on his face, but very pale. Gen walked up to her father, smiling. He always looked forward to Mike and Gen's visits and wanted so to feel well when they were there. He loved to kid Mike about that wedding night when he had chased Mike away from his bride.
"Where's Mike, Gen?" he asked her.
"I'm here, Dad," Mike answered.
"Well, don't get too close to me, you two. I don't know what I've got, and I might be giving it, you know."

Later that night, Gen heard her father getting out of bed and beginning the long walk down the hall to the bathroom. "I jumped out of bed and ran to him just as his legs gave way and he sprawled in the hall. The muscle relaxant that had been prescribed for him was too strong, I'm afraid. He couldn't control his body movement, and I struggled to lift him until Mike, awakened by the commotion, jumped up and ran to us. He took Dad's arms and just lifted him like a baby."

Gen sat beside her dying father for several days and tried to talk to him. "Mike and I finally had to return to Los Angeles to tape the programs that we had been delaying. We had only been home several days when Mom called and told us Dad had died.

"My mother and father always slept in a double bed. Mom was completely devoted to Dad. She seemed to live for her husband, and I believe it was because of that love and devotion that he lived to be ninety-six years old. He passed away during the night as he lay in that double bed beside mother. Just the way he would have wanted.

"Mike and I bought a tombstone bearing the Purnell family name. The four names of those who died were added to that tombstone only months apart. It was a tragedy, a disaster.

You can go for years untouched by death. Then, just when you think you've escaped, death pays its visit and takes away the ones you love."

From the large picture window in the Trafalgar Suite, Mike looked down at the lifeboat beneath them as he listened to Gen talk about the deaths in her family. The long, orange lifeboat had "Limit 50 Persons" stenciled on its side and round green containers marked "Water, Safe for Drinking" lashed to its hull. For a moment, the sun broke through the mist and reflected up on them from the sea.

"When the Titanic went down," said Mike, "during those last seconds afloat over a thousand people were simultaneously plunged into the icy waters to die. On our show we interviewed one of the survivors who remembered that moment well. The crewmen in charge of her lifeboat ordered the passengers to yell loudly and to hit the lifeboat with hands and feet as noisily as they could."

"Why?" asked Gen.

"Because it drowned out the sounds of death coming from the sinking liner," he replied.

Mike turned from the window and sat beside Gen on the sofa beneath a portrait of the Duke of Trafalgar, who died during the battle that bears his name.

"I've often thought about that moment on the Titanic when the cries of the dying were drowned out by the noises of those who would survive. I suppose it was a natural order for the crewmen to give, to protect the morale of those passengers fortunate enough to end up in the lifeboats, but I still resent it somehow. We try so hard to avoid the sounds or the sights of death and then, when they confront us, we aren't ready to deal with them.

"I know," remembered Mike, "because when death took Robert Fredrick Dowd from me, I wasn't ready or equipped to handle that moment in any way. He was five years my senior, and saw me as his kid brother until the day he died.

" 'OK, kid,' he would yell at me, 'Get out on the field and knock heads.' "

Michael Dowd was only seven, but his brother, Bob, was twelve, the most impressive sandlot football player in their tough Chicago neighborhood.

"I'm coming, Bob," Mike yelled, struggling to put on the old helmet his mother had bought for him at a neighbor's rummage sale.

Bob waited for a moment, then lifted the huddle and literally carried Mike to the scrimmage line.

"But, Bob, I don't have my helmet on. Mom will kill me if she comes out and finds me."

With one ear-bending scrunch, Bob placed the helmet on his little brother's head, placed the football in his hands, bent him over, and began the count.

"3, 7, 9, hike!" he called out. Michael hiked the ball, and was immediately buried in a pile of neighborhood bodies.

"My brother Bob always played football without a helmet," said Mike. "My mom gave up on him early in his backyard football career. I looked up to him with wide-eyed wonder. Bob was more father to me than brother. He was a strange, wonderful mix of both my parents—the gentle faith of my mom and the street-wise tough of my dad.

"I would hear an alarm clock go off every morning before the rest of our family even stirred. Bob would dress and disappear into the semidarkness. I was curious about his early morning journeys, and one morning I decided to follow him.

Bob Dowd tiptoed through the kitchen and down the back steps. Mike followed at a distance. His brother walked directly across their backyard and up Diversey Street. Still half-asleep, he had no idea he was being followed, so ten-year-old Michael Dowd went undetected. Bob hurried the last few blocks across Rosylyn and down Sycamore, and suddenly turned in through the gates of their neighborhood church.

Mike stood looking in the door at the handful of parishioners who had gathered to "break their fast" with the Holy Eucharist. In the hushed silence, he watched his brother walk up a side aisle of the church and slide across the pew to the center. Mike

*was impressed that Bob bowed to the cross before entering the
row and joining the neighbors who had gathered there.*

*"In the name of the Father, the Son, and the Holy Ghost,
let us pray."*

"Bob knelt and prayed at fifteen with the fervor of a saint,"
Mike recalled. "I watched him pray that day and on other
days through the years, and I wondered what drew him to
that place like a magnet. Perhaps he knew that death would
visit him sooner than the rest of us—I don't know. But every
morning of his life, with few exceptions, Bob began the day
at church in prayer.

"Dad liked Bob best," Mike admitted, "And I don't blame
him. Bob and Dad loved to play tag football or catch, while
I went off to hear the big bands or to dance in the Melody
Mill Ballroom. They couldn't understand why I was drawn
so to music and live performance, any more than I could understand why Bob was drawn to early-morning Mass. Still, we
loved each other."

Bob Dowd once pushed open the door to Michael's room
in a rage.

"I can't remember now what he was so angry about," said
Mike years later, "but after exercising his lungs in my direction
he let fly an open-handed punch that sent me sprawling.

" 'Bob Dowd, get out here right now,' my dad yelled at
my older brother. 'You can't run around this house yelling
and hitting people. Out to the shed with you.'

"My dad found me crying. I was almost as big as Bob then,
and easily as strong.

" 'Why do you let him push you around like that?' Dad
asked.

"I still can't answer his question," continued Mike Douglas.
"I just couldn't hit him back. I think I loved him too much.
Even when he did those natural sibling things, I loved him."

*The large, sloppy sign read, "VOTE BOB DOWD, COMMIS-
SIONER." Mike Douglas stood at the edge of the picnic crowd
in Forest Park, Illinois, and listened to his big brother's speech.*

Bob had become a tile and roofing specialist. He would work hard all day. But immediately when Forest Park kids got out of school, Bob would always be front and center at the city park, coaching Little League and Pop Warner football. He had never missed a season; he was a fanatic. He loved that little town just west of Chicago, and had invested much of his energy in the town and its people. Now Bob had decided to run for city commissioner.

"The parks are drying up. The baseball diamond is hard and dangerous. Kids' chins and kneecaps are skinned and bloody. It's time we invested in the youth of Forest Park. Vote Dowd. Vote Proud."

Mike joined in the laughter and the applause as his big brother climbed down off the park table and joined his neighbors for an election eve picnic.

"He doesn't have a chance," an old timer next to Mike mumbled. "Too many Krauts in this place."

"Forest Hill was predominantly German and Italian ethnic," explained Mike, "but the old-timer forgot one fact. Bob Dowd had been coaching the children of Forest Park for over a decade. They had all grown up and registered to vote. They remembered Coach Bob, and they elected him commissioner of Forest Park by a landslide.

"All the bunting and flags in the park that day reminded me of a similar moment fifteen years before. One night, after I had finished boot camp and my basic training in Chicago and was about to report to the training program in communications at the University of Wisconsin, my brother Bob showed up unexpectedly at my parents' home.

" 'Hi, kid. How ya doing?' he asked rather casually.

" 'Fine, Bob. What are you doing here?'

" 'Just passing through,' he answered, looking away.

" 'You old soft touch,' I kidded him. 'You've come to say good-bye.'

"I shouldn't have joked like that. It was one of those rare times when suddenly you discover that you are loved. He didn't speak much that night. The war was touch-and-go. A lot of lives were being lost, and a lot of ships were being sunk—and he knew all that. He just ate with us, chatted about his tile business, and turned in early.

"The next morning I watched my brother Bob, now a grown man, tiptoe through the kitchen and out the back screen door without making a sound to wake us. I knew where he was going. I pictured him walking across Diversey, down Rosylyn, and over Sycamore, through the gates of that little brownstone church. I lay in bed, picturing him bowing to the cross and then sliding into the pew. I knew that when the priest called the people to pray, my brother Bob would kneel, bow his head, and pray for me.

"Later my family gathered to say goodby. My brother stood on the edge of the crowd. I could see him standing there, waiting, feeling awkward and yet determined to show his love for me.

"At first he didn't say anything," Mike said, "but I could see in his eyes all the things he wanted to say. I remember he finally grabbed me and hugged me, and with tears streaming down his face he said, 'Take care of yourself, kid. I'll be praying for you.' It was perhaps the most eloquent farewell I'll ever know. Then he turned and walked away into the crowd without looking back."

"The Mike Douglas Show" was on remote location in Cypress Gardens, Florida. Mike was introducing a spectacular waterski review when his personal secretary ran up, telegram in hand.

"Mike, it's your brother," she whispered. "He's very ill."

Mike ran to a nearby pay phone and, hands shaking, he dialed Bob's home in Forest Park. His nephew answered. Bob's oldest son had suffered a serious head injury as a marine in Vietnam. He spoke with a strange kind of frankness when Mike asked about his brother.

"That gregarious Irishman is terminal," he said. That was it. Bob was dying, and something in Mike went crazy to see him before he died. Bob had sent him off in style when he

left boot camp. This was the last chance to pay him back. "This time," Mike thought, "I'll send him off in style with the same kind of love that he showered on me that day twenty-five years ago."

He ran to his location producer's trailer.

"My brother's dying, Woody, I'm on my way to Chicago."

"But Mike, we have . . ."

"I'm on my way now, Woody. Find somebody to fill in for me. This time nothing keeps me on location. This time nothing will get in my way."

"I was almost crying," remembered Mike, "barking orders to my secretary to call in an emergency high-priority air reservation, calling my driver to get the car in place, calling Gen to join me en route. I had to get to Chicago before he died. They had operated on his kidneys and found him full of cancer, and I hadn't even known he was sick.

"Finally, I landed at O'Hare, and a limousine whisked me to Forest Park. I ran up the stairs of the hospital and down those lonely corridors to his room. My dad was sitting in a chair at Bob's bed. I didn't even see him there at first. I simply charged across the room, threw my arms around Bob, and began to cry.

" 'My gosh,' he said, 'what a greeting from my little brother.'

" 'Are you all right?' I asked, and have hated myself for that dumb question to this day.

" 'I'm fine,' he answered with that best of all hospital lies. But he wasn't fine. And I couldn't stop the tears. I just sat there crying and holding him and remembering all the times that my schedule and his had kept us apart, wishing I had known him better.

"When visiting hours were over," Mike recounted, "my mom and dad and I sat in the living room of Bob's little home.

" 'That was nice, Mike,' my dad said to me.

" 'What was nice?' I answered.

" 'The way you hugged your brother Bob and cried.'

" 'Nice?' It was such a surprise to hear my father call that

spontaneous outpouring of love and guilt and fear 'nice.' I
was stunned. I sat there watching my dad in stunned silence.
Then suddenly I realized what he was saying. He could not
reach out to take his sons in his arms. He could not cry and
say 'I love you.' I could tell that night that Dad was saying
to me, 'Oh, Mike, if only I could have done that, too.' But
he couldn't. So he simply whispered to me, 'Mike, that was
nice.'

"Why do we freeze up around the ones we love? Why do
we let all the important things go unsaid?"

For a moment Mike was quiet. He walked to the window
of the Trafalgar Suite and stared again at the distant horizon.
The sun had disappeared once again behind the storm clouds,
and rain was rattling against the liner's metal skin.

"I would have given up every dime that I had acquired to
make Bob well. But the fortune I had made and the power I
had accumulated in the business were helpless to stop the
cancer that gnawed at Bob. In my room that night I finally
realized what people mean when they say, 'All you can do
is pray.' I hadn't built up a backlog of prayers like Bob had
through the years; I was still pretty much an amateur in the
prayer department. I was a crises pray-er, a foxhole believer.
I had prayed when I feared that my darling Gen would die
after giving birth to the twins. And I prayed briefly before
each show. But this prayer was different. My brother's life
hung in the balance. I knelt beside the bed and begged God
to heal him.

"The next day my sister-in-law, Eloise, showed me a letter
from Bob's doctors that stated he would probably die in sixty
days. The letter was to back a formal request by the family
to keep their youngest son out of the service now that his
father was terminally ill. The boy was needed to support his
family during that time of crisis, so I picked up the phone
and called Vice President Hubert Humphrey to make sure
the family's request would be granted. In his typically gracious
way, he promised to help and he followed through on that
promise.

"I returned to Florida to continue taping with both my

prayers and that letter promising Bob only sixty days to live rattling around in my brain. But Bob didn't die in sixty days. He made medical history, of sorts. They wrote his case up in a medical journal, crediting Bob's incredible will to live. He hung on for more than half a year, and I thanked God for every extra day Bob lived.

"I was taping when the last call came. The cast and crew were gathered around the coffee pot at a taping break when Eloise called. 'He's gone, Mike,' she said, with a kind of serenity that comes from watching someone you love die well. 'Thank God,' she added. 'He has been suffering so.'

"The next thing I knew, I was in Chicago again, walking past the casket of my brother. Sitting in the limousine that day a thousand memories of Bob and the time we had spent together played and replayed. I remembered his boxing my ears and kneeling to pray. I remembered him yelling at me in anger and throwing his arms around me in love. I remembered him towering above me with scorn over a dropped football and picking me up and carrying me home when I skinned my knee. He was my brother, and I loved him, and when he died something died in me.

"The people of Forest Park named their own local park and playground Dowd Park after my brother Bob. Occasionally when I am in the neighborhood I visit the park and watch the kids playing there. I think I would trade everything I have accomplished in show business to see my name up there. The celebrity I have attained, the power and the wealth and the honors are nothing in comparison to that sign hanging above Dowd Park. He loved the kids of that city, and the city remembered. I wonder if anyone will remember me?"

Mike moved out once more onto the balcony overlooking the sea. The great ship rolled with the North Atlantic surge and Mike Douglas stood alone, looking down at the lifeboat, remembering.

*Don't ever make the mistake of underestimating Lawrence Welk.
He is a perfect example of those men and women in the
entertainment business who have carefully developed a stage
personality that keeps his millions of fans humming along. But
the man is more than champagne bubbles and downbeat. He
is philosophical. He thinks about life and acts out of loyalty to
principles he finds important. He is a skilled administrator and
runs a tight ship. But more important, he cares about people.
I have dined with Lawrence or golfed with Lawrence when fans
approached us for autographs. I'll sign and head to my table
or the greens, but Lawrence may stay all day chatting with
his fans. He's just that kind of guy.*

MIKE DOUGLAS

And don't be afraid to make mistakes. Look on "failures" as
learning experiences and be grateful for them. Every
businessperson, including me, has had a long, long list of
failures. . . . I agree with George Hamid, the famous showman
who built the Steel Pier in Atlantic City, who said, "Whatever
success I've attained, I owe to my failures. A hungry showman
learns more from one resounding failure than he does from
two successes!" How true. I've often thought God sends us
hard spots and troubles deliberately, to teach and instruct, to
test our mettle, and to help us develop the strength of character
that lies idle in us. I can truthfully say that the hardships
and disappointments in my life helped me more than anything
else to achieve my goals.

LAWRENCE WELK

Chapter Ten

A QEII STEWARD IN STARCHED WHITES and gold braid knocked on the living room door of the Trafalgar Suite. Mike's personal secretary, Lynn Faragalli, opened the door. The steward held out a silver tray. On it was an envelope with the impressive monogram of Queen Elizabeth II. In artful handwritten script, the envelope was addressed to Mr. and Mrs. Mike Douglas. Lynn thanked the steward, who bowed slightly and disappeared down the long, silent corridor of Signal Deck.

Gen Douglas opened the engraved invitation which read, "Captain Douglas Ridley, R.D., RNR, requests the pleasure of your company for a reception in his private quarters at 5:30 on Saturday, the fifth of December. Your steward will direct you."

It was signed with a personal note of welcome by Douglas Ridley, Captain of the QEII.

"There are obvious privileges that accompany fame," Mike commented, "but in the long run there is more pain than privilege to being famous. Perhaps the worst price of fame is one's almost total lack of privacy. It is especially true for the performer in films or television whose face is seen and easily recognized by tens of millions of people. Add to that my being on television for twenty years, watched by millions every day, and it is almost impossible to go anywhere or do anything

181

without being recognized. But I guess that's the price you pay for success.

"Dad, can we see Mary Poppins *in a real theater this time— with popcorn and Cokes and everything?"*

Kelly Douglas was only eight, but already she was tired of private screenings in her home or at a studio. She wanted to go to a local movie house with her dad like all the other children in her school. Against his own better judgment, Mike agreed. The date was set. Father and daughter ventured out. There were no limousines, no private screenings, no perquisites of privilege—just a daughter and her dad on the town.

"We got in line with the rest of the people," Mike remembered. "Kelly was excited about being there with her dad. And I felt proud and a little giddy at being there myself. It was, I admit, a bit strange to stand in line and wait in the cold to see a picture when I knew that the producer, the director, even the stars of that film would have loved to put on a private screening of the film for Kelly and me in their homes or at the studio. They knew the value of my commenting on the film on 'The Mike Douglas Show.' They knew the publicity that would result from an interview, complete with film clips, before twenty million Americans. But Kelly was my daughter. There were few times that I could please her in little ways, and this was one of those wonderful times. At least, that's the way the Saturday afternoon adventure began.

"Suddenly, in the line of movie patrons, a woman shrieked. She literally screamed my name so that it echoed up and down the street," remembered Mike. " 'Mike Douglaaas!' she hollered again, until everybody in the line was craning to look in my direction. We were mobbed. 'Are you really Mike Douglas?' somebody asked. 'Will you autograph my popcorn box . . . my cast . . . my shirt sleeve?' others yelled at me. The line quickly dissolved into a mass of giggling, screaming, pushing parents and their kids. I don't exaggerate. It has happened many times and it's awful!

"Remember," Mike said, "sometimes asking for an autograph is strictly an excuse for getting really close to a famous
figure to check that person out firsthand. 'Does he have blue
eyes?' 'Is that his own hair?' 'Are his teeth real?' For some
strong, sick reason, the people want to touch you, too—even
to take something from you. In New York I was exiting a
Frank Sinatra concert with Gen, and a woman in the crowd
walked up to us, and ripped my shirt with one hand, jerking
off buttons with the other. It ruined my shirt and our evening.
I know my vocation is based on building and keeping loyal
fans, but when those same fans attack in person it can be
frightening and quite dangerous.

"In the last year we have had several entertainment celebrities shot or stabbed by deranged fans. President Reagan's
would-be assassin was really stalking a young movie star. It
is no wonder that, though dependent on fans, entertainment
personalities spend millions trying to protect themselves from
fans run amok. That day, in the movie line with Kelly, I
realized I had surrendered my rights to walk with anonymity
in the streets of my own town. The privacy of my wife and
family, too, had been jeopardized forever. We've spent a lifetime living with that reality and hating it.

"Little Kelly spilled her popcorn as the crowd shoved her
aside to get to me. I tried to grab her and keep her from
falling. Just that minute, the theater manager and several ush-
ers pushed the crowd aside to rescue us. In his office safely
inside the theater, the manager said, 'Mr. Douglas, you don't
have to stand in line here. You know that. In fact, we would
prefer you didn't. You understand don't you?'

"Of course I understood. It was humiliating to be lectured
by that well-meaning man on a subject I knew far better than
he. But I wanted to yell at him, 'Don't you realize, man,
my daughter wanted just once to stand in a normal line with
a normal daddy. Don't you realize how much I wanted it
for her—to make her happy, to help her feel just like her
little friends feel when they stand hand in hand with their
daddies?' Instead, I just thanked the manager, who gave Kelly

a *Sound of Music* cast album and a second box of popcorn and sneaked us out the back door of his theater.

"Several days later, Gen reported a painful conversation she had before school with Kelly.

" 'Mommy, are you going to pick me up at school today?' Kelly asked Gen.

" 'No, honey,' she answered. 'Daddy is coming with his driver to get you.'

" 'Please, Mom. You come. I don't want Daddy to pick me up. It makes too much fuss.'

"Kelly loved me," Mike affirmed, "but she was right. It wasn't fair to expose her to those same fans that can out of curiosity and naïvete victimize us both. But," Mike added, "it can really hurt me, as I know it hurt Kelly, to realize we could never do those normal things other parents and children can do."

Gen Douglas remembered the time her husband was appearing on the very popular interview program conducted by Phil Donahue. "He asked me to join Mike, other guests, and their wives before the cameras that day for informal chatter. I have an almost unbreakable rule," Gen continued, "that Mike is the performer and I am not. He is the public figure in our family. I will maintain my privacy for the both of us. I want to be able to walk the streets of my town and not risk being recognized and mobbed. But that day I broke the rule and went on the air, and though I enjoyed the experience, I paid a price in my own loss of privacy for doing it.

"I believe that it is my job to shut the doors on the world and create a safe and loving space where my family and I can truly be at home, private, cut off from the pressures of this most-pressured business. Some people think celebrities buy big houses simply to impress. In fact, many of us buy big houses because it's the only safe space we have to walk around in. We are, in some crazy ways, prisoners of our own success. There are certain restaurants and shops and athletic clubs where we can escape safely into the real world, but for the most part our only safe and comfortable space is our home.

So we invest in those homes, building an environment that leads to building a family and keeping that family safe and together against a business that could tear us apart."

"In London," Mike added, "before we boarded the QEII, Gen and I had one of those very rare experiences of walking the streets together without being recognized. Although my show is catching on in Europe, I am primarily an American-based entertainer. I am not widely recognized in foreign cities. So Gen and I went shopping in London. We ate bangers and tomatoes in a little cafeteria on Wesley Street. We held hands and bought souvenirs and played like tourists. No one recognized me. It was wonderful."

Mike's valet emerged from the deep double closets of the QEII's Trafalgar Suite with Mike's tuxedo for the reception in Captain Ridley's private quarters. He removed a freshly starched and ironed tuxedo shirt from its box, and assembled studs and cuff links to match. Mike walked in from the bathroom, and the valet helped him dress for the evening event, as he had helped Mike through six different changes of clothing for that busy videotaping day.

"I resented the valet's presence at first," Gen spoke frankly in the sitting room nearby. "As Mike's schedule increased, as his fame grew, I was robbed of some of those natural tasks a woman can perform for her man. In those early days I ironed his tuxedo shirt, the only one he had. I patched his pants and darned his socks. I was everything then: cook, maid, baby-sitter, business partner, creative consultant, counselor, makeup artist, and valet. Little by little, I had to give up many of those tasks that helped hold us together, that made me important to Mike. Women's Liberation might criticize me for confessing it, but I needed to be needed. I liked being needed. At first it was difficult for me to let go of my old jobs, and early on I resented each of the people who took my place. I felt robbed of those wifely prerogatives that were the early glue to our relationship.

"Then I began to find new ways to aid Mike," Gen continued. "Instead of competing with those brought in to help Mike survive the heavy pressure, I saw them as my friends and allies. They were, after all, taking pressure off me as well. So, I found myself free to be Mike's equal and partner and friend, not just his cook or his valet. I found that I, too, had trustworthy intuitions about the entertainment business. I found I, too, could read the trade papers and keep up on what was happening in Mike's world so I could be knowledgeable when we discussed the difficult and demanding decisions he had to make. I found I was artistic, and could create living environments that would begin and end our day together with peace and comfort and joy.

"What we were both discovering during those early days of Mike's success was that fame put awful pressures on our relationships, and that maintaining those relationships required energy and creativity and a willingness to compromise, to change, to give up old jobs and take on new. As Mike's fame grew, so grew the pressures on us as a couple and as a family. As Mike's schedule and pace grew more and more demanding, we had to determine more and more firmly that nothing would destroy the love we felt for each other and for our children. It has not been easy."

The twins, Christine and Michele, stood in the living room of Mike and Gen's little tract home in Los Angeles. It was 1960. Woody Frazer had just called with the good news that Mike was chosen by Westinghouse to be the host on their new Cleveland talk show. But for the girls it was not good news.

"Mom, we've been moving back and forth across the country all our lives. We don't want to move again."

Both Gen and Mike remember well that day twenty-one years ago, when their girls were sophomores in a Los Angeles high school. As they held their crying daughters, they had to admit that all those moves back and forth across the country had been difficult if not unfair to those two young girls.

"We had checked the schools in Cleveland," remembered Gen, "and knew they were good schools. We knew our daughters could be happy there, but they loved their boarding school in California and wanted desperately to stay. At the same time, I knew Mike's career was in the balance. He was picking up guest spots around the country. He was tired of saloon singing and one-time television appearances. We both wanted to settle down. Cleveland was our hope for that, but our daughters would not easily be convinced. So we took a terrible risk. We compromised; we let our daughters stay in their California boarding school and we moved to Cleveland. We risked losing our relationship with the twins in order to maintain it."

Mike and Gen Douglas stood in the airport concourse before that flight to Cleveland knowing they were leaving two young daughters behind. For a moment the four of them, with little Kelly close by, held each other close and cried. Then, Mike and Gen boarded the plane, and the twins turned and walked away.

"I was torn in pieces," Gen remembered, "but I had to take the chance. To simply order the girls to move with us would have been robbing them of their own free will. To abandon my husband or to make him sacrifice this big chance in his vocation would have been to threaten his future and ours. So, we compromised, praying that the decision would be right and that one day we would be united as a family again. Within a year both girls joined us in Cleveland, and were happily enrolled in their new school in Lakewood, Ohio. Within a year we were a family again.

"We've been married almost forty years now," Gen said, "and we've worked hard to maintain our relationship—both of us have. Mike lives in a world of fame and adulation. There isn't a day that passes that some young actress doesn't throw herself at Mike. I see them so often pulling their coats open, throwing their arms around Mike, and giving him a big hug.

At first Mike and I were jealous at different times of each other; it works both ways. Then you grow up. You tell yourself it's natural. A man is going to be attracted to other women. Women are going to be attracted to other men. So both of us work at being attractive to each other.

"Let's face it," Gen affirmed, "usually a man is attracted first to a woman because of her beauty. Hopefully, his attraction grows to appreciate the person within—to what lies behind the physical beauty. But a woman's beauty goes on forever being important to a man. We mow our lawns and landscape to make our grounds more attractive. We pick our flowers and put them in a vase to make the house inside more full of color and beauty. Why shouldn't the person inside the house look attractive too? Looks aren't everything. You don't have to be pretty to be very successful at marriage. But I still believe it helps to look as pretty as you can for your man as he rushes off to work, and as he returns to your arms at the end of the day. It isn't the requirement for love, but I think it nurtures it.

"The other day Mike said to me, 'Gen, when you come in that door, the whole room lights up.' It was one of those wonderful moments when Mike, with just a sentence, can make it all worthwhile. He knows how hard I work on staying attractive to him. He appreciates it, and works hard to stay attractive to me. It takes effort to maintain a marriage. For almost forty years we've been making that effort—in good times and in bad. I think the times of depression or hardships are the times we become closer. I don't know how to explain it. Our love just feels more meaningful when we really need each other's strength to get us through the crises. Hard work and loyalty are two basic rules for us. We are loyal to each other over everything and everybody else. When we feel fear or jealousy creeping up—when communications break down—then we sit down together and talk about it, whatever it is. We work it out.

"Children can be a real problem here. A mother especially

risks letting her children become her whole life. Often I have chosen Mike over the children, leaving them with a competent and loving sitter, so that I could go on the road with my husband and be with him when he felt the natural pressures a man feels on the road. I knew I wasn't going to have my children forever, but I was determined to have Mike. So I did my best to prepare my children to grow up, giving them love and encouraging them to make their own lives, while I worked to keep my life with Mike creative and growing and alive."

Mike and Gen Douglas were led to the Captain's private elevator on board the QEII. A beautiful young dancer from the ship's entertainment company passed Mike as they stood waiting for the lift. With wide, ingénue eyes, she approached Mike for an autograph and kissed him when he obliged. Gen winked and smiled. Mike looked sheepish.

A ship's officer announced Mike and Gen to the Captain. He immediately turned from the small party of regular voyagers to whom he had been chatting and greeted the Douglases. A steward carried trays of drinks, while a stewardess presided over hors d'oeuvres that included lobster and caviar and liver paté.

The Captain's cabin was small in comparison to the Trafalgar Suite. In a position of honor on the wall was a picture of the first Queen Elizabeth, with its four beautiful orange smokestacks gleaming in the sun, surrounded by a bevy of tugboats guiding her out of Southampton Harbor. Walls and tables of the cabin were covered with exotic memorabilia—Asian artifacts, including Japanese books and Chinese screens in inlaid ivory and teak, and folk art from the Caribbean. There were also historic navigation books and charts, and instruments in brass. In the cabin were a handful of other guests, including a countess from Wales and a member of Parliament.

Entertaining and being entertained was business as usual for the Douglases. Sometimes it was, in fact, as Gen confessed later, another of the prices they had to pay for fame. "It's hard, sometimes, to know when people seem interested in us if they really are interested at all. Agents and lawyers and managers; celebrities, politicians, and stars have all kinds of reasons for wanting to be with Mike," Gen said. "Some want to get themselves or somebody they know on the show. Some want to have their picture taken and used in personal publicity or in a paper or magazine. Some want to be close, just to tell their friends they met a star. If you aren't careful, you can get suspicious of everybody. That leads to having no friends at all."

"Having friends in this business isn't easy," added Mike. "In fact, losing friends seems another price we pay to achieve in entertainment. It's difficult to be in one place long enough to build friendships. You try to keep old friendships going with those fifty-dollar phone calls across the Atlantic or across the country. You try to get back to Cleveland or to Philadelphia or to New York to visit old friends and catch them up and be caught up by them, but time passes, and friendships die, and you end up in parties like this one pretending you care about the people in the room and daydreaming about the real friends you let get away."

The ship's photographer entered Captain Ridley's cabin and lined up guests for a portrait. "The ship was rolling," Mike remembered later, "and we were high on the topmost deck of the QEII and could feel every roll. I looked around the room as we lined up for that picture, and everybody was swaying but the Captain. His legs worked like shock absorbers keeping him level while the rest of us leaned back and forth in unison. When we got into position for the picture, the Captain stood still and the rest of us kept bumping into him. I suppose there is a comparison in my business. Somehow, over the years, you just get conditioned to the stormy weather and learn to ride it out."

Back in the Trafalgar Suite later, Mike and Gen sat with their shoes off, reminiscing about the stormy business they were in and the other prices they had had to pay to succeed in that business.

"I suppose to talk of fame without talking about the work it takes would be unfair," Mike began. "Unlike a lot of people who can leave their work after eight or ten hours of it, my work stays with me twenty-four hours a day. I wake up in the middle of the night thinking about it. I'm really a good sleeper, ordinarily, but if there's something on an upcoming show that doesn't feel just right, if the chemistry is flat, my mind works on bringing a show to life until it happens.

"It looks easy, just I and my guests chatting away about this subject or that. But the façade is a lie. Every guest represents a different kind of expertise. I have staff members who will research a biography on a guest, read articles about him or books she has written. Then they give me thumbnail sketches to work with, but they are never enough. I end up reading everything, including the books an author guest has written. Just being on the air, getting in and out of clothing and makeup, rehearsing, and getting ready for the next day's show is a full day's work. But I have to read hundreds of pages a day, make notes, check back over research, oversee the scheduling of future guests, and keep the business and technical wheels greased as well. It never ends.

"People are talking about the death of the talk show," added Mike defensively, "but that's a lot of rubbish. There will always be a place for quality talk. The problem is, we're in a period now where the same guests are being asked the same questions by everyone. It's a bore. There's no adventure, no risk, no discovery. There are approximately four-hundred-sixty-six local television talk shows being aired today. The only way to rise above the mass with something special is to work harder and longer and more creatively than all the rest."

"Hey, Mike, the ratings are down in Atlanta," the young producer said. "Better go to work on that."

Mike Douglas was hurrying through the halls of his television

*production studio. Apparently, one of his producers had just
read the nightly rating book in Atlanta, and Mike's share of
the audience was not up high as they hoped.*

*The producers and the ad agency people met in Mike's office
that day for a briefing. Nightly ratings in all the major markets
were scanned. Mike's show had the highest rating in daytime
television history in New York and Chicago and Los Angeles
that week, but in Atlanta the very same show had not scored
high in the rating game.*

*"Mike," said one producer worriedly, "we need Atlanta. It's
the flagship of southern television. Our sponsors watch Atlanta
like a hawk."*

*"But, Joe," Mike replied, "ratings aren't always accurate.
Look at what the same show did everywhere else."*

*"I know, but we need Atlanta. Don't you have some excuse
to get down there and stir up the loyal fans and bring new
fans on board?"*

*Mike thought. He'd been in so many conversations like that
one. He knew the rules: "It isn't enough to produce; you have
to promote." There was no time for a trip to Atlanta, but there
was the need to go.*

*"Yes, I have an excuse, Joe. Doug Sanders has been asking
me to play the Atlanta Golf Classic, and he has a big charity
event for ten thousand people in the arena there. Besides, they're
doing "That Was the Week That Was" on location there, and
I've been asked to do a guest spot on it."*

*"Great," the producer agreed. "Get down there and pull those
ratings up."*

"Ratings mean life or death in this business," said Mike.
"I hate the ratings game, but I'm forced, like everybody else,
to play it. It's as much a part of my work as creating programs.
My show can be excellent, an Emmy-award winner, but if
nobody watches it, or if a few million short of our goal watch
it, we're in trouble.

"So I went to Atlanta," Mike recalled. "I played in the

Atlanta Golf Classic, I did the guest spot on "That Was the Week That Was," and then I lined up with other celebrities backstage at the arena for a walk-on appearance and a song. Westinghouse, my producer at the time, had representatives traveling with me. They needed the ratings hike. They had sold the commercials, and commercials go for the price that ratings dictate. So when they saw one little ratings drop in Atlanta, down we went, entourage and all, to bring the ratings back up again.

"When I walked out on that Atlanta stage, the crowd went wild. Backstage again, I questioned the wisdom of the Group W representatives' loyalty to the ratings system. The people of Atlanta knew me. They could only know me through "The Mike Douglas Show." It was obvious from their enthusiasm that they were watching it. It wasn't six months before we were number one in Atlanta. A drop of several points in the ratings game, and everybody panicked. That's the business I'm in. Lose a city, lose a nation, lose a career in broadcasting. You work twenty-four hours a day to guarantee that doesn't happen.

"So the schedule is divided between producing and promoting. Picture it. We spend most of the week in the studio from early morning until early evening. We spend the evening reading and writing for the next day's show. And on weekends we're off to places like Atlanta for promotional tours or on-location shots. It never ends. And the energy it requires," added Mike, "is really something."

Mike Douglas sat in his dressing room on Sound Stage 5 in Hollywood. His makeup man, Jim Ruffino, had just administered the final touch to Mike's artificial tan for the day. Dayton Anderson had dressed his boss in the properly color-coordinated slacks, jacket, shirt, and tie scheduled for that day's first program. Lynn Faragalli, Mike's personal secretary, ran in messages from agency people and Mike's production staff. Mike had just flown in that morning from Miami, where he had

*been given an award for public service by the National Academy
of Television Arts and Sciences, Miami Chapter.*
*"We have a little hold-up, Mike." Stuart Crowner, Mike's
talent coordinator for the "Mike Douglas Entertainment Hour,"
entered with the news that a guest artist's music was missing,
but that substitute charts were on their way. It would mean a
fifteen-minute delay.*
*"That fifteen minutes will cost us thousands," Mike grum-
bled, knowing that Crowner's estimate meant thirty minutes,
not fifteen.*

"Always double somebody's time estimate," Mike said with
a knowing grin. "They try to protect me, to keep me from
losing the pace. But I own this show. I know what every
minute costs to rent these facilities and to keep cast and crew
in place. I have to produce energy to administer the show,
and more energy to get out there and do it.
"I have my own methods for getting ready for a show,"
Mike added. "The adrenaline has to flow or I'm flat. If I'm
flat even the band can feel it. I train myself like an athlete
or a fighter going into the ring."
"I don't know where energy comes from," he mused. "I
know God blessed me with more than my share. But it is
still easy to see why people in this business get addicted to
drugs or to booze to keep their energy levels flowing. You
read about the drug-related deaths in this business. Young
talents like John Belushi or Janis Joplin or Joe Cocker have
to get their systems up far higher than I do: they have to fill
great arenas with their energy. So they turn to synthetic energy
sources."

*Lynn Faragalli set a large glass of orange juice on the table
before Mike. He swallowed a handful of vitamins, and drank
the juice. For a moment they conversed about a controversial
question on Mike's second show, a book Mike needed to scan
before the taping two hours away, and a call from Gen about*

the dinner and screening party they were hosting for a charity that night.

Stuart Crowner appeared again. This time Mike's director was in tow.

"What's happening, guys?" Mike asked nervously. "We've got three shows to tape today, and we haven't even started on the first one."

"I'm sorry, Mike," the director apologized, "but the lighting guys are going nuts trying to cover the jazz dance number. Those dancers are all over the place. Won't be long now, though." Both men turned and disappeared.

"How do you double 'won't be long'?" Mike asked. "The technical guys need terrific energy to get through a day, just like the performers. Then, when the day ends, especially on location, when your mind is racing and your body is tied up with nervous tension, you have to find some kind of release. That's one of the reasons there's so much crazy sex in our trade, and partying and smoking pot and taking tranquilizers like Valium. We get our systems traveling at such a rapid pace it is difficult to cool them down."

"Two minutes, Mike," Crowner appeared for a third time, then disappeared again. Ruffino touched up Mike's makeup. Tape machines were whirling. Guests were in place. The studio audience was watching the sign that would signal their cue to applaud. Mike Douglas stood behind a long brown curtain. Lights blinked over the stage door: "Mike Douglas Taping."

"And now, ladies and gentlemen, our host, Mr. Mike Douglas."

The band played a fanfare. Mike paused to make the sign of the cross, then plunged into sixty minutes of self-imposed pressure.

"I don't know why I keep performing," Mike confessed as he relaxed on the sofa of the Trafalgar Suite sitting room.

"I don't think it's for the money. There is some mysterious driving force in me that never lets me stop. Something in me is driven to strive for improvement, and to fight against anything that gets in improvement's way. I don't believe in luck. And I don't believe God comes riding down a moonbeam and does special favors for a few of us. I believe I've made my own breaks by working hard and by not quitting when every bone in my body wanted to quit.

"There may be luck, good fortune, or wonderful timing in this business, when the right thing happens at the right place at the right time with no apparent effort or planning. Woody Frazer's invitation to come to Cleveland was that way for me. But most of the breaks you make by staying in there when your back aches and your brain is begging you to lie down and die. I knocked on doors for fifteen years. I sang in saloons and shopping-center openings and ladies'-club benefits until my tonsils were sore. I've had a lot more downs than ups in this business. I've walked through a lot more valleys than I have scaled mountaintops, but you just can't quit trying. That's the real price of fame—hard work. Nothing else will do it."

Mike yawned and stood up, stretching. It was late, time to begin making preparations for sleep. Then he remembered a new song he was scheduled to sing during the next morning's taping with Ben Vereen.

"Have you seen those lyrics, honey?" Mike asked, rummaging through the pile of scripts nearby.

"It's on the coffee table, Mike," she answered from the dressing room, "under tomorrow's taping schedule."

Mike sat down on the sofa to scan the lyrics. He had memorized more than three thousand songs and could sing almost any one of them on cue. That night he was memorizing song number three thousand one.

"I truly love this business," he had said earlier. "And I'll probably always be a part of it in some way or other. If I ever reach the point I can't perform, I'll be performing in my heart. Sure, it costs us in so many different ways to be famous. But I don't perform with fame or its costs in mind. I perform because I am a performer, full of the music and the blarney of Ireland, I suppose. I picture that when I'm old and decrepit, if anybody asks, I'll still pop a line or tell a story or get up and sing a song to anybody who will listen. I'll never stop—unless it costs me Gen. That price I wouldn't pay. I'd stop entertaining before I'd lose that woman. I'll pay almost any price but that one."

Billy Graham is a very special man. Like millions of people around the globe, I have been mesmerized by his presence. He has all the charismatic traits of a great leader, but he is a man. He is not perfect, nor does he pretend to be. In my interviews with Graham I have been comforted and instructed by his humanness. He has made mistakes and has been held accountable by the world's press in some very tough interviews. But unlike so many who have reached that pinnacle of fame and influence, Graham is quick to confess his failures and to ask forgiveness for them. That takes a truly great person. I am convinced that his ability to confess and be forgiven so graciously by his fellow men comes out of his practice of confessing to and being forgiven by God.

MIKE DOUGLAS

The American people are yearning for answers to the deeper issues of life—answers which can only be found in God. There is a spiritual hunger in this nation. . . . Almost everywhere I go—an airplane, a hotel lobby, a restaurant, a television studio—I have people of all kinds come up to me and unburden their hearts. Their stories, of course, are different, and yet there is a common theme: "I have a fine home, a good job, and economic security. But down inside I am empty. I need God. How can I find Him and fill the hunger in my heart? . . ." There is only one way to speak to the spiritual hunger of this age. It is the same way Christians throughout the centuries have spoken to the spiritual yearnings of every age— by pointing people to Christ.

BILLY GRAHAM

Chapter Eleven

THE FIVE-HUNDRED-THIRTY-SIX-SEAT THEATER on the upper deck of the QEII plays first-run movies during the North-Atlantic crossing. There are also lectures, concerts, travelogues, and amateur reviews during the long days at sea. But on Sunday the room was transformed. A communion table, draped with a British flag, sat stage center. At the door, ship stewards distributed orange Anglican prayer books inscribed in gold with the words, "Divine service for use in Cunard Ships." The QEII's organist played one of Wesley's hymns as passengers gathered for worship.

"There was a lovely huge spray of mums and tiger lilies before the altar," Gen Douglas recalled later, "and, just before the service began, the officers of the QEII entered wearing full dress uniforms and took their places in the front row directly in front of the ship's old, carved wooden pulpit. It is tradition that on the high seas the ship's master, Captain Ridley, leads the worship."

"God is spirit, and those who worship him must worship him in spirit and truth. . . ."

"The Captain wore gold braid," Gen recalled, "and opened the worship with rather stiff, British formality. The service seemed a million miles away from Oklahoma City and the

202 MIKE DOUGLAS: When the Going Gets Tough

First Christian Church I attended every Sunday morning of my childhood. I remember sitting on a cold, enamel table in our family kitchen after my Saturday night bath, preparing for the following Sunday ritual. Mom would heat up the curling iron, curl my hair, and put a big bow in it. Fresh bread and an apple pie or chocolate cake would be baking in the oven for our Sunday dinner. The kitchen was warm and fragrant and full of faith.

"It would not have crossed my mother's mind to miss Sunday school or church. My two brothers and I often thought about it, but were afraid to suggest the idea. So every Sunday morning was the same for the Purnell family. After breakfast we walked the six or seven blocks to church. At the door, Mom distributed the offering money, kissed us each on the cheek, and saw us off to Sunday school. At five minutes to eleven, we met to sit together, in the third row on the right side, for worship.

"My religious experience as a child was quite different from Gen's," Mike remembered. "In fact, the service on board the QEII that day was not unlike the worship I knew as an Irish Catholic living in that tough ethnic ghetto in old Chicago. But Gen and I have similar *parental* traditions. My mom marched us off to Mass every Sunday morning, too, even during those cold Chicago winter mornings when our offering coins froze to our fingers and our faces were red and frostbitten before we slid into the pews. Often our teeth were still chattering when we bowed before the cross as the procession entered at the call to worship."

Captain Ridley led the congregation in the general confession: "Almighty and most merciful Father; we have erred and strayed from thy ways like lost sheep. We have followed too much the devices and desires of our own hearts. We have offended against thy holy laws. We have left undone those things which we ought to have done; and we have done those things which we ought not to have done. And there is no health in us. Have mercy upon us, Lord. Spare

*us who confess our faults. Restore those who are penitent.
According to thy promises declared unto mankind in Christ
Jesus our Lord. And grant, O most merciful Father, for
his sake, that we may hereafter live a godly, righteous and
sober life. To the glory of thy holy name, Amen."*

"In our little church in Oklahoma City," Gen remembered,
"there was no gold cross or hand-carved altar or brocade-
covered kneelers. There was a rough wooden mourners' bench.
At the end of each service, the pastor would invite all of us
who needed forgiveness to come forward and confess our sins
at the altar. While the congregation sang, "Just as I am, without
one plea . . . O Lamb of God, I come," people would quietly
walk from their pews and kneel to pray. At the close of the
service, friends would gather around the altar and those praying there in a kind of circle of concern. Then everyone would
hug and cry and go home for fried chicken and hominy grits.
I never really felt sinful as a child, but I recall going to that
altar one Sunday evening, praying with a group of friends
gathered around me, and feeling surrounded by God's love
and his people's."

"There's where we were different," interrupted Mike, grinning. "I did sin as a child, and I felt it. One sin I remember
vividly cost me a lot more than a trip to the altar for confession
to get it forgiven.

"I was twelve. I had passed the carved wooden Indian
chained to the front of McCormick's Cigar and Smokes Shop
a hundred times. This time, however, I stopped to stare in
the window at the boxes full of imported cigars, the brightly
colored tobacco tins, and the wall of handcarved pipes—one
with a stem as long as my arm. I can't remember why I entered
McCormick's store that day; I think I was after an empty
cigar box to decorate for a school project," Mike remembered
hazily, "and when old McCormick turned to enter the back
room in search of one, I grabbed up a fat Havana cigar and
ran from the shop."

Dad Dowd was out of town that weekend. Mike hid the

cigar in his father's little supply shed behind their flat, and waited until late afternoon when his mother was shopping. Then he crept into the darkness of the shed, lit up the thick Havana cigar, and tried his best to smoke it.

"I don't know how I got it lit that day," Mike said later, "but somehow I managed to light and eventually to smoke the whole cigar. The room was full of blue haze. My clothing stank of acrid smoke, and almost immediately after my gasping, snorting triumph I began to feel deathly ill."

Mrs. Dowd walked up the sidewalk, her arms full of groceries from the old Ford's trunk, when Michael ran from the shed and began to throw up into the pansies that bordered the backyard.

"What's the matter, Michael?" Ma Dowd cried at him, dropping her groceries and running to assist her son. "Are you ill? . . ."

One whiff of Michael's clothing, and the story didn't need to be told.

She waited until Michael was quite finished and quite pale, then she asked quietly, "Michael, where did you get those cigarettes?"

"It was a cigar, Mom. Havana. I got it at McCormick's," Mike answered, glad his father was out of town, and hoping his mother would not betray him.

"And how did you get the cigar, Michael?" she asked, her voice gaining a steely edge as the truth that Michael had stolen it quickly dawned.

"I just took it, Mom," Michael confessed.

Suddenly, she turned him around and marched him towards the car.

"Where are we going, Ma?" he asked, knowing full well their destination and already beginning to dread it.

"You, not we, are going to McCormick's to confess your sin and ask for his forgiveness."

"But Mom," Mike groaned, "aren't you going in with me?"

"I wasn't with you when you took it, was I?" she replied. "It is your crime, Michael. You must pay for it as you committed it, alone."

"I walked into McCormick's a twelve-year-old," Mike remembered, "and I came out forty-seven. I've never stolen again. McCormick forgave me, especially with mom's quarter in his pocket, but that still wasn't enough for that Irish Catholic mother of mine. On Sunday morning, when we knelt in that brownstone neighborhood church and the priest said, "Almighty and merciful Father, we have sinned against thy laws," my mother looked across the pew at me, her lips mouthing in unison that ancient confession with mine. When the priest shared the promise of forgiveness, she smiled at me, looked back at her lectionary, and began to pray. I knew I had really been forgiven then."

"O, Lord, we beseech thee to hear the prayers of those who confess their sins unto thee; that they, whose consciences by sin are accused, by the merciful pardon may be forgiven; through Christ our Lord. Amen."

"My mother taught me one of the most important lessons of my life, that weekend," Mike affirmed. "We live in an untruthful world, where everybody lies and cheats and connives to get where they're going. Not everybody, perhaps, but in my experience practically everybody, lies. Everybody has larceny in them. The most pious of us lies from time to time. If only my mom had had her way in all of us, there never would have been a Watergate. I was such a fan of President Nixon. But Watergate was stupid. Why couldn't he have been honest? What a way to be remembered in life. You see it on his face. The man looks miserable. He looks a thousand years old now. How much better he would have been if he had just been honest. Whatever the price of that truthfulness, it would have been worth it.

"I've been in trouble with certain members of the press all my life because I tell the truth as I know it. I think that day in McCormick's, facing a man by myself to confess that I had lied and stolen, and seeking his forgiveness, was one of the great preventatives against continuing those sins in my life. I could be a good liar, because I have an excellent memory. You have to have an excellent memory to be a good liar, you know. I'd rather just tell the truth and take my lumps. I've been that way since I was twelve, and I am grateful for the woman who refused to let me get away with the little lie, knowing that one day the big lies would destroy me."

Somewhere in the stormy North Atlantic, passengers on the QEII heard Captain Ridley say, "O, Lord, open thou our lips," and in unison the congregation answered, "And our mouth shall shew forth thy praise."

"Frankly," Gen confessed after that Sunday worship at sea, "there were good times and there were bad times in my church in Oklahoma City. We lived in a 'dry' town. You couldn't buy liquor legally in the city limits. And the church had strict standards against drinking and smoking—even dancing was prohibited. But church people said one thing on Sunday and did something else the rest of the week. The churchly standards were consistently broken by everyone, including the string of ministers we had while I was growing into adulthood. One pastor was caught by a deacon with liquor in his car. Another minister had an affair with our church organist. Both were fired. I spent years being angry at the church for its double standards. They called people to worship God with their whole heart, and then I watched those same people consistently fall far short of that goal.

"But as I grew older I had to give up my anger at the church. Those Christians were after all, just people, imperfect like me. They often struggled with problems far more serious than could be easily solved; often they were confused and confounded by life."

Again Captain Ridley intoned the words of that ancient liturgy, "O God make speed to save us." And the passenger congregation echoed in reply, "O Lord make haste to help us."

"I finally realized," Gen continued, "that it wasn't my job to judge others, but to follow Christ in the best way I could follow him. I had no business getting sidetracked by others' failures. I had one job—to work on overcoming my own failures and acting out my faith in ways that were my own."

"I was only seventeen when I married Mike and joined his parents in Chicago while we awaited his return from war. Mike's parents were Catholic. I had never been inside a Catholic church before. In Oklahoma City there was obvious prejudice against the few Catholics in our town. I remember still the awful stories my neighborhood friends told me about the tiny convent in downtown Oklahoma City. 'They live in cells, like jail cells,' one friend told me. 'And they never come out. Somebody sticks bread and water under their door and they just live in that cell all their lives.'

"Later I learned that convent was the home of a small order of nuns who worked with the poor and homeless in our city. Yet by the time I reached Chicago at the ripe old age of seventeen, I too had inherited some of that anti-Catholic prejudice from my conservative Protestant playmates.

"The first Sunday in Chicago, Mom and Dad Dowd invited me to attend worship in Mike's church. I went with my stomach full of butterflies. But minutes after I joined that little congregation of Irish Catholic Christians, I felt at home. They knelt to pray at their altar like we had knelt to pray. They sang hymns of praise like the hymns and choruses we had sung. And they confessed Jesus their Savior and Lord, just like my Baptist friends in Oklahoma City had confessed Him. The service was very reverent. The sunlight streamed in the stained-glass windows. The organ played quietly and the choir in the balcony, no better than our amateur choir at home, sang with enthusiasm the hymns of worship and the responses to prayer.

"I'll never forget that first Sunday afternoon when I discovered that Catholics loved Jesus just like my Protestant friends. When I wrote Mom and Dad in Oklahoma City, telling them about my secret marriage to Mike, I told them that Mike's family were Catholic and that I would be worshiping with them while I waited for Mike in Chicago. I didn't know what Mom and Dad would reply. Finally, their answer came: 'Dear Sis. We are happy for you and Mike, and we are glad that you are worshiping with the Dowds. Remember always, Gen, that there is only one God, and that everywhere you go there will be people who worship him in different ways. Don't be afraid to go on worshiping him in your own way alongside them.' "

"Glory be to the Father, and to the Son, and to the Holy Spirit; As it was in the beginning, is now, and ever shall be; world without end. Amen."

"God gave me a gift to entertain people," Mike said. "I thank him for that gift every day. But there are times I wonder if he knew what developing and maintaining that gift would cost us both in terms of time. There's hardly a Sunday goes by that Gen and I aren't on the road somewhere far from home. In the past few years we've done remote shows all over the country, as well as in Moscow and Monaco, in London and Paris, and now here on the North Atlantic. You can't be regular, faithful churchgoers with a schedule like ours, yet, to be faithful to our schedule is to be faithful to the gift he has given me. Therefore, much of my worship has to be in dressing rooms or television studios, on planes and ships and trains."

"In the name of the Father, the Son, and the Holy Ghost, let us pray."

Mike Douglas stood in his dressing room on Sound Stage 5 in Hollywood. The page signaled that he was due on his entry marks in one minute. Slowly he scanned the copy for his opening lines, replaced the copy in its folder, made the sign of the cross and walked, with only seconds to spare, to the waiting cameras. It is the same; this last second before taping routine, whether Douglas is at his home studios in Hollywood, on location in Moscow, or on board the QEII on the high seas. Mike prays silently and crosses himself. Then, and only then, he will begin a taping.

"I am a God-fearing man," Mike affirmed. "I know that may sound self-serving. 'God-fearing' has become in common parlance a synonym for religious. For me," he explained, "it means more than that—much more. I really do fear God. I see him with awe and wonder. I believe him to be the creator and sustainer of the universe. He is my creator, as well. He cares about the planet whirling through space, but he cares about me, too—insignificant, tiny me. He has given me the talent that I have and the life and the energy to use that talent. When I stop just before a program begins, it is to honor God, to salute him, to acknowledge him as Lord of my life.

"I don't know how prayer works," Mike confessed. "When I prayed for God to heal my brother, he answered with six months of life beyond what the doctors had predicted, but Bob wasn't healed. When Gen was blind from an allergic reaction to anticonvulsant drugs after giving birth to the twins, I prayed just as sincerely, and in days she was seeing normally again. I suppose, too, I'll never know why God answers certain prayers and seems to ignore others. All I know for certain is that his son, our Lord, asked us to pray without ceasing. So, whatever happens, I pray. Sometimes my shows are terrible, even after I have prayed that they might go well. Other times, sure losers turn out as Emmy nominees. So, up times or down, I continue to acknowledge God in prayer. How he answers me is in his hands, not mine."

"Our Father, who art in heaven, hallowed be thy name. Thy kingdom come. Thy will be done, on earth as it is

*in heaven. Give us this day, our daily bread, and forgive
us our debts as we forgive our debtors. And lead us not
into temptation, but deliver us from evil. For thine is the
kingdom and the power, and the glory forever. Amen!*

Sunday morning, Gen Douglas sat in the Trafalgar Suite
still wearing her diamond and emerald cross. "For the first
twenty years, Mike and I lived on very little money and a
whole lot of dreams. When we finally succeeded in this business,
I decided to create a beautiful piece of jewelry that would
be a wonderful sign both of God's gifts to us and of our commitment and gratitude to him. I hope that generation after generation of my children and their children will have this cross as
a memory and as a reminder.

*Captain Ridley opened the chapel Bible of the QEII. "Today's
lesson," he began, "is taken from Paul to the Romans, chapter
fifteen. 'We who are strong, let each of us please his neighbor
for his good. For Christ did not please himself. . . .' "*

"In my experience," said Mike, "often the people who have
moved me with their faithfulness are people who may not be
hung up on the outward trappings, but who have something
within. Of course, a part of worship is to join the congregation
of believers and sing and pray and put money in the basket
when it passes. But another—and I think as significant a part
of worship—is to serve and love your neighbor on the road,
by your example, not just by your words.

"I had a great uncle who was very serious about his Christian
faith, but who seldom discussed it with anyone. He had a
neighbor who was a real reprobate. The man was foul-mouthed,
tore down my uncle's fencing just as an act of spite, tossed
garbage into his backyard, and generally made a terrible, despi-
cable neighbor of himself.

"My uncle never fought back. Whenever the neighbor acted
out of anger, my uncle replied by loving him, by giving the

old man gifts, and by repairing the damage the neighbor had done without recrimination or revenge. One day the neighbor melted under my uncle's love. His Christian charity had been, as the Bible says, 'Coals of fire heaped on the enemies' head.' The neighbor, without a word of explanation, simply asked my uncle to forgive him and, weeping, he went about repairing all the damage he had done to my uncle's place.

"That's the Christian faith as I believe it. One man living it out before another man until that man sees Christ in the other's life. Not necessarily long sermons, nor books and tracts to pass out, nor Bible-thumping over the backyard fence. Just obeying Christ's command, 'Love your neighbor as yourself.' That's what it takes. Those are the people who have changed my life."

"May the God of steadfastness and encouragement grant you to live in such harmony with one another in accord with Christ Jesus, that together you may with one voice glorify the Lord. . . . For I tell you that Christ became a servant to show God's truthfulness, to confirm the promises. . . ."

Gen Douglas walks her mother slowly up the walk from the Douglas guest house to the bright and cheery breakfast room where Mike and Gen begin each day. The backyard is a profusion of flowers, and Gramma Purnell stops to admire a bed of red and yellow tulips. For a moment, the two women chat. Then they continue the slow, laborious morning walk to breakfast.

"We read about Christ becoming our servant," said Gen, "but it is easy to forget that he has commanded us to be the servant of others as well. Mom is eighty-eight. Half a century has passed since she welcomed Michael into the kitchen the day I first met him. She is still full of life, but at her age, so many of the old systems have broken down. She can't function as well as she used to. In many ways she is as dependent on me now as I was dependent on her as a child. Sometimes that isn't easy for Mike and me, with our travel and production schedule. But we both see it as one small way of acting out the commands of Christ to serve others.

"There's another, selfish side of taking care of your parents when they're old. If we put our parents away, our children watch and remember. The example we live out before them in treating our parents with love and regard is the example they will follow in treating us when we reach old age. If we mistreat our parents or ignore them in their time of need, our children notice that as well. The example we set may be our own doing."

"It isn't easy," admitted Gen. "In a way, it seems like you have another child. Most times she's a fine addition to our home. But when someone reaches eighty-eight, you have to understand that every day is not going to be perfect. That person is not going to be as sharp as she was in days past. Sometimes you have to repeat yourself three or four times. You have to say, 'Now, Mother, I don't want you asking questions, then forgetting the answer immediately. I know, we both forget things, but let's try to remember this time, O.K.?' You really have to correct and love a lot. You have to be patient and kind when you feel like shouting. Isn't that all part of being a servant, as Jesus commanded us?

"After breakfast Mom loves to return to her guest cottage and watch the religious television programs, especially Dr. Robert Schuller preaching from his glass church in Anaheim. Later in the afternoon, after reading the Sunday *Times* and crocheting or knitting, she joins us in the main house for conversation and for dinner. I say keeping her in our home instead of committing her to some kind of institution for the old and the infirm is an act of servanthood, but in fact she still contributes to our life as much as we contribute to hers. And after investing her life in ours, it would be such a shame to not return our love to her as payment for her investment."

"My brother, Bob, was a real servant," Mike added. "I suppose his death was one of the times I felt farthest from, and, at the same time, closest to God. I just have to believe that God needed Bob or he wouldn't have taken him. He was so good as a Christian believer, so consistent in faith and action. He gave his life to other people. He was really a servant of the people of his town, of his neighbors.

"I don't feel I've done enough for other people," confessed Mike, "and I intend to rectify that someday in my life. I don't know when. Maybe when I stop paying attention to this stupid success syndrome that is so basic to the entertainment industry, to every vocation I suppose."

"Lord have mercy upon us," Captain Ridley prays.
"Christ, have mercy upon us," the congregation answers.

"Mike feels guilty that so much of his time has to be spent on his own productions," Gen explained. "He admires his brother Bob for giving so much of his time away. But Mike is generous with his time, too. In the last few years Mike has been recognized for his personal work by groups as varied as the Catholic Apostolate of Radio, Boys' Town of Italy, the National Father's Day Council, and the Juvenile Diabetes Foundation. Mike's grandmother, Elizabeth Brady, died from diabetes. This year Mike is the national chairperson of the American Diabetes Association. He is constantly on the go for one charity or the other as a national promoter or sponsor, or making celebrity guest appearances for benefits and fund drives and telethons. He says he does little for people, but in fact he works very hard contributing to the welfare of others."

"Almighty God, Father of all mercies, we thine unworthy servants do give thee most humble and hearty thanks for all thy goodness and loving kindness to us and to all people. We bless thee for our creation, preservation and all the blessings of this life, but above all, for thine inestimable

love in the redemption of the world by our Lord Jesus
Christ; for the means of grace and for the hope of glory.
And, we beseech thee, give us that due sense of all thy
mercies that our hearts may be unfeignedly thankful, and
that we show forth thy praise, not only with our lips, but
in our lives; by walking before thee in holiness and right-
eousness all our days; through Jesus Christ our Lord, to
whom with thee and the Holy Ghost be all honor and glory,
world without end, Amen."

"Gen and I have so much to be grateful for. But I don't
say that because we live in one of the five great houses of
Los Angeles or have success in a very competitive business.
Those things, the material things, aren't the important things
in life. Sometimes I look at all the affluence. I see people trying
to outdo one another, to make themselves look more important
than their neighbors. It all seems so silly to me. And it makes
me so very happy that my youngest daughter spent those for-
mative years in Philadelphia, attending the right kinds of
schools and living the right kind of life.

"We don't live in terribly modest surroundings, but the false
virtues of affluence and power become less and less important
to me every day. I realize Gen and I have all the comforts
of life and it is easy to say we could sacrifice them, but I
don't feel I've ever really lost my old values, even with the
material things we have accumulated. I'd be satisfied to live
the way I used to live, in a little GI house. I really would.
You know, having the best house, the best furniture, the best
car, the best clothes doesn't mean that much to me any more.

"I don't know when that change came about in my life.
It's funny, you get caught up in the success syndrome. You
struggle. You may not be the best father in the world because
you're devoting so much of your time to improving your status
in life, so that you can provide things for your family that
you didn't have as a youngster. And then, suddenly, you get
all of those things. I never had a new car; I always bought a

used one. Then suddenly you're able to go in and buy a car
and write a check and drive out—it's paid for. You're able
to buy things, not charge them. And all of a sudden those
things don't mean that much. I find that I got more of a
charge out of some of the used cars I bought than I get out
of the new ones. It's funny how the values change as you go
on in life. All of those things become less and less important.

"The change is almost undetectable. Suddenly, you begin
to think about the gift of life and about the God who gives
it. You begin to see yourself caught up in a whirl of your
own making. You begin to realize that people are more important than projects, but that you spend most of your time on
projects, not people. Little by little you change; your values
flip-flop; you look back and wish you could do it all again."

*The crew of the QEII, her officers and personnel, joined with
the congregation of passengers to sing the closing hymn.*

"*O Trinity of love and power,
Our brethren shield in danger's hour.
From rock and tempest, fire and foe,
Protect them wheresoe'er they go;
Thus evermore shall rise to Thee
Glad hymns of praise from land and sea.*"

"I wish I could have Jesus on my television program," Mike
remarked after the service. "I wish I could ask him the questions I have about life and death. I picture him as very striking-
looking, with very sharp features. I imagine he has a wonderful
beard and wonderful soft, long hair, the way I've seen him
in holy pictures. I fantasize that he has piercing eyes—understanding eyes—and a tranquil look on his face.

"I picture him sitting across from me on "The Mike Douglas
Show." I am looking right at him, talking to him like I talk
to all my guests. (I never have been able to talk to anybody
unless I look into their eyes.)

"I suppose I'd thank him first, for everything that he has done for me, for Gen, for our family. Then I'd simply ask him why? 'Why, Lord, why?' And I suppose I'd spend the rest of eternity listening, finally understanding what is such a mystery to me now."

Captain Ridley stood one last time before the QEII worshipers that day. He closed his prayer book, lifted his hand in blessing and gave the final grace:
"The grace of our Lord Jesus Christ, and the love of God, and the fellowship of the Holy Ghost, be with us all evermore. Amen."

Mike and Gen Douglas joined prayerfully in that "Amen."

I just read a full-page, full-color ad in Time *magazine featuring Ted "Captain Outrageous" Turner at the helm of his America's-Cup-winning yacht. The headline reads, "Here's to gut feelings and those who still follow them." To interview Ted Turner is to discover there are still dreams that come true and dreamers who dream them. He listens to the critics and the skeptics and then he acts on his dreams. He turned WTBS-TV in Atlanta into a "superstation" using communication satellites. He founded Cable News Network, the world's first twenty-four-hour news network. He bought the Atlanta Braves and moved them out of last place. In one interview he stated his view of leadership in three short bursts: "Lead, follow, or get out of the way." When the going gets tough, Turner really gets going.*

MIKE DOUGLAS

It doesn't bother me that I'm committing almost all I have to the Cable News Network. Had I known I was going to fail when I started, I would still have done it because it needs to be done. . . . Of course, I also think we'll make a fortune.

TED TURNER

I just read a full-page, full-color ad in Time *magazine featuring Ted "Captain Outrageous" Turner at the helm of his America's-Cup-winning yacht. The headline reads, "Here's to gut feelings and those who still follow them." To interview Ted Turner is to discover there are still dreams that come true and dreamers who dream them. He listens to the critics and the skeptics and then he acts on his dreams. He turned WTBS-TV in Atlanta into a "superstation" using communication satellites. He founded Cable News Network, the world's first twenty-four-hour news network. He bought the Atlanta Braves and moved them out of last place. In one interview he stated his view of leadership in three short bursts: "Lead, follow, or get out of the way." When the going gets tough, Turner really gets going.*

MIKE DOUGLAS

It doesn't bother me that I'm committing almost all I have to the Cable News Network. Had I known I was going to fail when I started, I would still have done it because it needs to be done. . . . Of course, I also think we'll make a fortune.

TED TURNER

Chapter Twelve

TUGBOATS DARTED OUT from Manhattan's harbor to guide the Queen Elizabeth II gently into her berth. The New York City skyline slowly hove into view. Two miles of electronic cable had been stowed. The Double Down Room showed no signs of the feverish activity that had filled it during the past five days of television taping. The "Mike Douglas Entertainment Hour" crew joined passengers lined up along the decks for their first sighting of Lady Liberty's torch held high in welcome. Mike and Gen Douglas stood on the private outdoor patio of the Trafalgar Suite watching the city lights dancing on the dark harbor waters.

"There are tranquil moments, even in our lives," Mike remarked later. "That was one of them. The great ship glided silently into port. No one on the decks below us was talking. Each person was lost in his or her own arrival reveries. Gen and I stood holding hands in the darkness, never dreaming that events only hours away would completely change our life and send us once more on the road."

U.S. customs would not allow the Douglas party off the ship until morning, because no customs officials were available for disembarking in the night. No phone lines would be strung to the ship until docking was complete and the Douglases had retired for the evening.

The QEII nudged into her downtown Manhattan berth. The

crowd of passengers, still wearing tuxedos from the evening's dinner and entertainment events, wandered to their cabins, feeling strange that they could be so close to being home yet still not disembark. The Mike Douglas crew, more than twenty-five of them, were chatting in groups around the ship, talking about the schedule for remote tapings in Hawaii the next few days, and wondering how they would get to Los Angeles, visit friends and family, and still make it to the airport to begin another on-location tour with Mike and the "Entertainment Hour." Mike and his crew had no idea that within a short time events would conspire to cancel the Hawaii tapings, to close down the "Mike Douglas Entertainment Hour."

"Within a few short weeks," Gen Douglas said later, "we had to give notices to almost our entire production team. Many of our crew had been with Mike since Cleveland, most since Philadelphia. After Westinghouse, Mike had invested heavily in the new "Mike Douglas Show" format. One of the reasons he wanted to stay in production was to keep our loyal crew together. They had given their talent to Mike over the years, and though Mike had paid well for that talent, he still felt indebted to each of them. It is not unlike a company owner who sees his business failing, wants to keep his employees together and working, but without cash flow cannot sustain the losses.

"We kept as many on the payroll as we could. But the others had to be notified that the show was being canceled. Mike sent individual letters to every crew member on that list expressing his gratitude for the years of loyal service. Unfortunately, there was no time to get everybody together. We were separated immediately from staffers who because of the rapid schedules in our business were off to Washington, D.C. or to Boston or to San Francisco on their new assignments. The others who couldn't find work immediately suffered the most.

"They are still like our children to us," Gen claimed. "We watch the trade papers for news of their new positions. We are concerned about what they're doing, and hope their profes-

sional and personal lives go well. After that, there is little
we can do. Remember," she added, "Mike was out of business
too, with losses of millions besides. And, regardless of rumors
to the contrary, nobody sustains the loss of millions of dollars
painlessly."

Mike didn't sleep well that last night on the QEII berthed
at New York's pier ten. He thought at first it was the loss
of movement with the ship lashed down firmly to the dock
instead of tossing in the stormy North Atlantic waters. But
it was also because his business sense had been questioning
the wisdom of trusting so much to the syndicators. Now that
the pressure of the QEII tapings was over, his mind began
to work on the business side of the entertainment industry
again.

"When we entered the library of our Beverly Hills home
just a few days after the cruise," Mike remembered later, "my
business manager and my lawyer were there with the bad
news."

"The rather stony faces of our associates signaled the serious-
ness of our losses," Gen remembered. "Mike's show had been
a winner, but sometimes being a winner is not enough. Attor-
neys and business managers, syndicators and ad agencies blame
one another and then blame the creative talent for the predica-
ment. But, in fact, when losses are discovered in this business
you have to correct your course rapidly with little time for
recrimination. Not only that—while the dust is still settling,
you have to decide whether that was your last big risk or if
you are willing to take another. Mike recovers faster than
anyone I've ever met.

"A Canadian broadcast group from Vancouver were already
on record wanting to cofinance, in their beautiful new studios,
four-and-a-half million dollars' worth of new 'Mike Douglas
Entertainment Hour' programs. We were doing preproduction
work on a television pilot with Burt Reynolds, Goldie Hawn,
and Kenny Rogers. They wanted Mike to finance the pilot
and estimated forty-five-thousand dollars more to get it in the
can. Mike laughed off the proposal with his warning that,

'When people say forty-five thousand, they mean a hundred thousand, and that's a lot of risk on top of the losses we've just sustained.' Other producers wanted Mike, and Mike was interested in doing more theatrical films—even in exploring the possibility of a Broadway show.

"Standing on the deck that last night in Manhattan, I could almost hear the overtures echoing up from Broadway," remembered Mike. "I love television, but I still have the urge to act. The toughest thing about this business is not *getting* to the top. It's *staying* there. You have to be alive to new challenges every day.

"There are times I ask myself, 'Why, Mike, are you going through all this again?' It's hard for me to explain my willingness, my obsession with twenty-four-hour schedules, the constant pressure, the tremendous risk. I know it isn't only the money or the material rewards. There's just some driving force in some of us that others don't have. There is something that keeps some people striving for improvement, for a better position in life. I don't know how to describe it. I just wake up in the morning feeling it. I often wonder if it would be easier to wake up in the morning satisfied, but I've given up trying to be different. God made me the way I am; so I'll just go on managing the crazy ambition, the bubbling energy, and developing the talents I've received from him."

In their library at the close of that fateful meeting with their associates, Mike decided that the "Entertainment Hour" would close, at least temporarily, and go out of production. The conversation then suddenly turned to the new dimensions of television, and to what lay ahead in television's future. Someone walked to the monitor in Mike's television room and turned on Ted Turner's Cable News Network broadcast.

"He's on with the news twenty-four hours a day, Mike. He is on cable, and he's plugging into America's homes by the tens of thousands every day. He is live on satellite to his stations, and he's providing many channels of news, information, and entertainment to those subscribers."

"We knew Ted Turner," Mike recalled later. "That Atlanta

wunderkind had transformed his little station into a globe-girdling cable power. Even the networks were trembling at Ted Turner's audacity and his creativity. He has been losing millions of dollars every month on his twenty-four-hour news network as a calculated risk to unseat the stranglehold the networks had on news delivery. Turner did not inherit those millions. He made them by risking. He took over a bankrupt business and made a fortune."

". . . And he knows about Mike Douglas," Gen added from her leather seat in the library.

"That's right," Mike's business manager cut in. " 'The Mike Douglas Show' was on Turner's Atlanta station, and did so well in the ratings that a network affiliate lured the program away. We did even better ratings there, and Turner was impressed."

"If I were Ted Turner," continued Gen, "the smartest move I could make right now is to sign up Mike to head up the entertainment end of his cable system. Mike has twenty years' experience in this business. Turner knows how valuable that experience could be to him."

The conversation stopped. "There have been moments of truth in my years in the entertainment business," Mike explained later, "when the obvious jumps up and waves and screams and makes itself known to everybody." Telephone lines between Los Angeles, New York, and Atlanta were hard-pressed those next few days as a deal was negotiated between Mike Douglas and Ted Turner's Cable News Network.

"Ted Turner is amazing," Mike recalled of their first face-to-face meeting. "He had just flown back from interviewing Castro in Cuba and played us a videotape of that interview. Turner's office was alive with energy. To walk through his massive broadcast studios is to see television's future. New ideas flow around that place like water from an artesian spring. There's no idea too outrageous for Turner to consider. He listens, asks questions, and decides—just like that. No hemming and hawing for Ted. Like he says, 'Lead, follow, or get out of the way.' "

"When Reese Schonfeld walked us into Ted Turner's office," Gen remembered, "he got up from his desk, grabbed us both in a bear hug, and said, 'Hey, glad to have you as part of the family.' Mike will be doing a live interview show every night at ten o'clock that will be telecast by satellite to the entire cable network. He will be producing five-to-eight entertainment specials a year as well. He'll have the chance to be a part of the news, too, with his first assignment to cover the Masters' Golf Tournament in Augusta, Georgia."

"We went to sleep that last night on the Queen Elizabeth II never dreaming that in a few short days we would be closing down the 'Mike Douglas Entertainment Hour,' with millions of dollars of losses, and signing up to broadcast a live, daily program for Ted Turner's Cable Network, or that Westinghouse would drop John Davidson the day we disembarked. The changes in this business come and go so fast," Mike said, shaking his head, "that you could get whiplash just trying to follow the action."

Customs officers were scheduled to begin disembarking QEII passengers at nine o'clock the next morning. Mike and Gen had one last meal in the Queen's Grill before being escorted to a V.I.P. customs office. Over grilled bangers and stewed tomatoes, a British breakfast tradition Mike still only tolerates, the Douglases talked about the future.

"All my life," recalled Mike, "I've wanted to do a television special on the subject of success. Success means something different to every individual. You see, I look upon my brother as being vastly more successful than I. The big houses or the millions of dollars I've made don't mean success to me. Success is something inside you. Success is the good things that people do for other people.

"My brother, Bob, did so many good things for so many people. He thought about himself last. He was more giving— much more giving and much less selfish—than I. Oh, people say, 'But look at what you've accomplished, Mike; look at what you've acquired. Look at the houses and the buildings and the real estate. You could afford to lose millions and still not be hurt terribly.' They may be right, but those accomplishments and acquisitions still don't equal success to me."

"Yes, but Mike," Gen interrupted, "in the last stage of Bob's life you helped him. You cleared up the bills that were left. You called Vice President Humphrey to be sure Bob's son wouldn't be sent to Vietnam when he was needed by Eloise. Remember, Bob's generosity left him nothing in reserve for himself."

"Honey," Mike answered, "What I'm saying is this. When Bob's church took up a collection, when they needed money for a mission or for a building project, Bob would put himself down for a thousand dollars, maybe more. He couldn't afford that. But somehow he would always come through. He knew his family needed the money, so he worked doubly hard to come through for God and for his family. Bob was generous. Bob was loving. Bob was a success. I wonder if I'll ever get free enough of this success syndrome I'm in to succeed at life as he has.

"When I die, I hope people will remember me as a man who gave of himself to make others a bit happier. I want them to remember me as somebody who made a lot of people smile. Hopefully, I make my viewers' days a bit easier, a bit brighter. I don't know what kind of mark I'm going to leave, if any mark at all. I don't know how I'll be remembered. There'll be a couple of old records around that nobody'll care about. The public forgets so quickly. Maybe they'll remember me for five minutes. Maybe they'll say, 'He was a nice guy, one of the nicer guys in show business.' Then they'll forget. Let's face it, the world will go on without me.

"I'm so envious of people who write, who create. It must be wonderful to be a George Gershwin and leave the world with all those wonderful melodies and lyrics. That's important to me. Leave the world with something, like my brother did."

The Douglas baggage had been checked through customs early that morning. A ship's officer escorted Mike and Gen to the private customs area. Passports were stamped. Purchases from overseas were declared. And Mike and Gen Douglas were guided down the long stairway to the disembarking dock, through the crowd of reporters, tourists, and Cunard officials, and to their waiting limousine. Mike and Gen rode through the streets of Manhattan en route to Kennedy Airport for their transcontinental flight to Los Angeles.

"There's a call for you, Mr. Douglas," said the chauffeur, "from your business manager, Mr. Andrews. You can get it on the car phone near your left elbow."

"Good morning, Vinnie. This is Mike. What's up?"

Gen Douglas knew from the pain in her husband's voice that the news Vinnie Andrews was conveying was serious. She had no idea at that moment just how serious it was— that the "Entertainment Hour" would soon be terminated. But from the look in Mike's eyes, she knew the news was bad. She reached across the back seat of that long studio limousine and took her husband's hand. They had survived bad news before. They would survive it again.

Addendum

JUST WEEKS AFTER MIKE AND GEN DOUGLAS left the QEII to face their own tough times, the British Government informed the Cunard Lines that their great ship had been drafted. The Queen Elizabeth II would serve as a troop carrier to ferry men of the Fifth Infantry Brigade to the conflict in the Falkland Islands. Working through the night, the crew transformed the QEII from luxury liner to troop ship. Plywood covered priceless tapestries and handloomed carpets; bone china, antique furniture, gold framed paintings and marble sculptures were removed. Narrow bunkbeds were hung in place of king-size stateroom beds. Helicopter landing pads were installed over swimming pools and entertainment decks. Beer and chips were hauled on board to replace stores of champagne and caviar.

Seventeen hundred passengers who had planned to sail the Queen to the warm, peaceful waters of the Mediterranean were turned away, and four thousand soldiers boarded the ship for that eight-thousand mile voyage to the war-torn waters of the icy South Atlantic. A few disgruntled passengers complained as they first heard news of their canceled vacation plans. "We had no adequate warning," one groaned when the great ship sailed away without them. But, as Mike and Gen Douglas know too well, there is never adequate warning for those times when the going really gets tough.